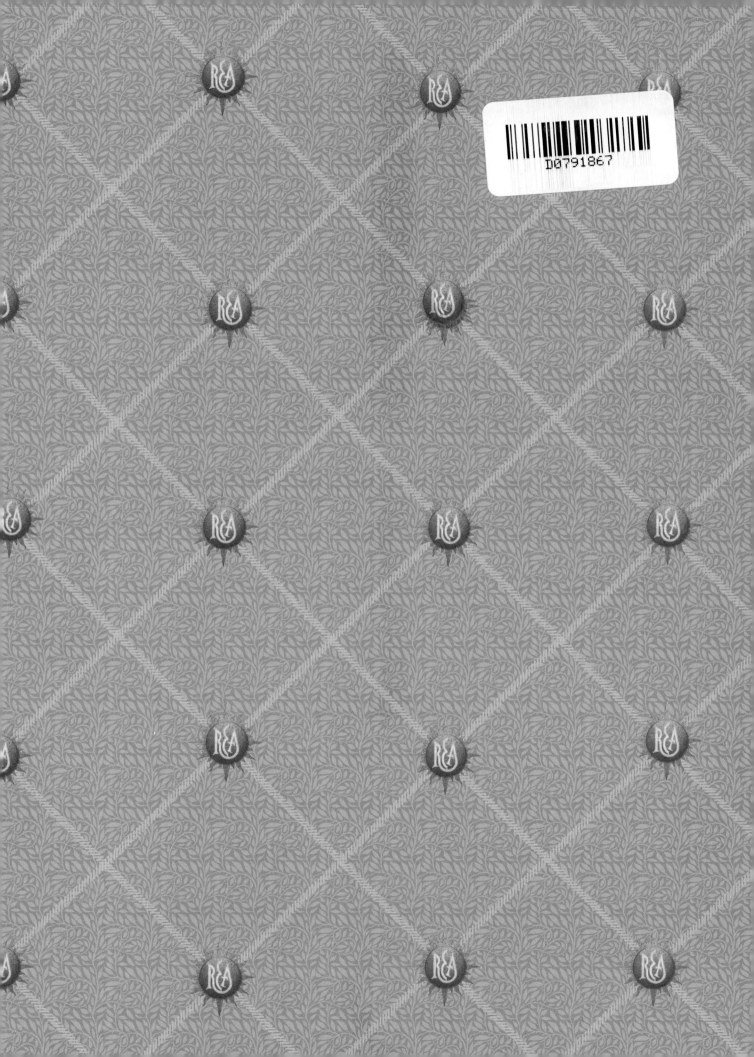

# QUEEN CREEK
# OLIVE MILL

## FAMILY COOKBOOK

### THE REA FAMILY

PERRY, BRENDA, SYDNEY, ESTE, JOEY, ANGELO, AND JOHN

The Reas at home: John, Sydney, Este, Perry, Brenda, Joey, Angelo.

ISBN 978-1-4675-3967-8

www.queencreekolivemill.com

25062 South Meridian Road, Queen Creek AZ 85142


DESIGNER/EDITOR/PRODUCER
Carol Haralson, Sedona, Arizona

PHOTOGRAPHY Janise Witt, Sedona, Arizona

BOOK LIAISON Sydney Rea


Printed in Canada

# INTRODUCTION

OVER A BOTTLE OF RED WINE and dinner in Birmingham, Michigan, we were pondering the direction our lives were taking. Perry's Italian heritage and passion for cooking led to the crazy idea of growing olive trees for the production of extra virgin olive oil. Why was nobody in America doing this? A handful of producers in California was it for domestically produced olive oil.

With an understanding of the health benefits of a Mediterranean olive oil based diet, and the knowledge of how to cook delicious meals with this healthy oil, the decision to go for it came before the end of the bottle of red.

Within one year of that night and after much research, we had moved our four children (and one on the way) to Phoenix, Arizona, and had planted our first grove of olive trees.

Fifteen years later, the Queen Creek Olive Mill is a thriving gathering spot for locals and visitors alike with the olive groves, mill, marketplace, and café. People ask all the time for the recipes used at the restaurant and in our home cooking. We decided it was time to put some of these popular dishes down in writing. The *Queen Creek Olive Mill Family Cookbook* is a compilation of recipes used at the Mill and in our family kitchen. We are happy to be able to pass down our family traditions to our children and at the same time to be able to share them with all of our friends. —PERRY AND BRENDA REA

SO, A LOT OF YOU MAY BE WONDERING. . . who exactly are these people? I could go into a long saga about our family history, but I will spare you the unnecessary details. There are three major things you need to know: We are a big family, we are an American-Canadian family of Italian descent (on my dad's side), and we love to eat. Growing up in a house with five children, I have become accustomed to the multi-course, three-hour-long family dinner that can spring out at you any day of the week. Although my mother, Brenda, works very hard in our kitchen, I am going to have to attribute the area of culinary expertise to my dad, Perry, or as he calls himself, "Master Blender."

The Rea family at the Mill: Sydney, Brenda, John, Perry, Angelo, Joey, Este.

We moved from Detroit to Phoenix when I was about seven years old. I had zero idea at the time what was going on, all I knew is that we were moving to a place where there were palm trees, and that was okay in my book. It took me a few years to realize the gravity of the dream my parents had when deciding to just pick up, move across the country, and establish an olive oil empire in the middle of the desert. My dad likes to refer to this as the point in his life when he switched "from motor oil to olive oil." (Clever, right? He loves this line). Anyway, for the rest of my childhood education I was instructed to give olive oil to my teachers as their present before Christmas break, and I thought this was so strange. No big red apple or bottle of perfume. I never understood why their eyes would fill with such excitement when I handed them the simple gift box filled with our extra virgin olive oil and balsamic vinegar. It was all a mystery to me.

Fast-forward about ten years and my understanding of the world finally began to fall into place while I was studying abroad in Florence, Italy. Cooking has always been second nature to me, and I think to every other kid in the Rea family. We were born and raised surrounded by pasta and red wine—how could we not know that you need garlic and olive oil in order to make anything and everything taste good?

Surprisingly, not every person is aware of this; my roommates were a prime example. I taught them the importance of a little drizzle of olive oil in every meal of the day. "Yes, you can use olive oil to cook your eggs…" "What!?" It finally dawned on me that not every 20-year-old American girl grew up in a family where they don't want to go out to dinner. Where Daddy's wood-oven pizza not only rivals, but squashes any other pizza within 4,000 miles.

Basically, what I want to let you know is how extremely lucky you are to be able to have access to these recipes. This is not just food, it is culinary heaven. I guarantee obsession with every dish my dad has chosen to include within the next couple of hundred or so pages.

You're welcome, and enjoy. — ESTE REA

From the blossom to the bottle: The Reas' Queen Creek Olive Mill in Queen Creek, Arizona produces hand-crafted extra virgin olive oil using nine varieties of olives.

EXTRA VIRGIN

REAS. OLIVE

ARIZONA

www.re

TUSCAN ESTATE

EXTRA VIRGIN OLIVE OIL

Arizona grown Pendolino, Grapolo, Lucca, Frantoio and Mission olives and California early harvest Mission olives are gently cold pressed. Perry Rea our master-blender hand crafts his award winning signature Extra Virgin Olive Oil with a fruity start, a grassy aroma and a peppery finish.

250 ml $10.⁴⁹
500 ml $15.⁹⁹
1 Gal $64.⁹⁹

Best of the Valley

DODGE

ANTIPAST

# Aperitivo Party

WE HAVE BEEN HOSTING APERITIVO
PARTIES AT OUR HOME FOR MANY YEARS.
FAST, EASY, AND QUICK-PREP ANTIPASTI,
GOOD WINE, FRIENDS AND FAMILY ARE
ALL YOU NEED TO CREATE YOUR OWN
APERITIVO GATHERING. DON'T BE
AFRAID TO SUBSTITUTE OTHER HANDY
INGREDIENTS IF THE ONES SPECIFIED
IN THE RECIPES ARE UNAVAILABLE.
HAVE FUN WITH THIS!

BRUSCHETTA STARTS WITH A BAGUETTE CUT INTO THREE-QUARTER-INCH THICK SLICES. THE SLICES ARE GRILLED OR TOASTED ON BOTH SIDES, THEN RUBBED LIBERALLY WITH A FRESHLY CUT CLOVE OF RAW GARLIC. TOPPING POSSIBILITIES ARE NEARLY ENDLESS. DON'T FORGET TO FINISH WITH A DRIZZLE OF EXTRA VIRGIN OLIVE OIL.

# Bruschetta Ideas

**CLOCKWISE FROM UPPER LEFT:**

**PEAR AND GOAT CHEESE** A dollop of goat cheese topped with sliced pear and a drizzle of QCOM Aged Balsamic Vinegar

**CHARDONNAY HERB MASCARPONE AND GREEN APPLE** Chardonnay Herb Mascarpone (page 20) topped with sliced green apple, finished with QCOM Fig Balsamic Vinegar

**BURNT MOZZARELLA AND PESTO** Sliced baguettes covered with grated whole milk mozzarella and broiled until bubbly and lightly browned, finished with Pesto del Piero (page 23)

**MASCARPONE WITH PROSCIUTTO AND CARAMELIZED RED ONION** QCOM Caramelized Red Onion and Fig Tapenade on a bed of mascarpone cheese, topped with very thinly sliced and rolled prosciutto

# Hummus

THIS IS OUR TAKE ON THE TRADITIONAL HEALTHY MEDITERRANEAN CHICKPEA DIP. TRY MAKING IT WITH QUEEN CREEK OLIVE MILL CHILI OLIVE OIL, LEMON OLIVE OIL, OR BLOOD ORANGE OLIVE OIL FOR AN INTERESTING TWIST.

1   fifteen-ounce can garbanzo beans (chickpeas) with half their liquid, or 2 cups cooked dried garbanzos with some of the cooking liquid

2   cloves garlic, peeled, coarsely chopped

2   tablespoons soy sauce

3   tablespoons freshly squeezed lemon juice

3   tablespoons extra virgin olive oil

3   tablespoons Tahini (sesame paste)

BLEND all ingredients, including reserved bean liquid, in a food processor until smooth. For bruschetta, pair the hummus with cucumber and roasted red peppers or with black olives and fresh sweet red peppers.

# Chardonnay Herb Mascarpone

THIS WONDERFUL CHEESE SPREAD CAN BE USED AS A BRUSCHETTA TOPPING OR ON AN ANTIPASTI PLATE.

8   ounces mascarpone cheese

2   tablespoons Chardonnay wine

2   teaspoons dried garlic chips

½   teaspoon dried oregano

½   teaspoon dried basil flakes

¼   teaspoon red chili flakes

½   teaspoon sea salt

MIX the cheese and wine in a medium bowl. Incorporate the garlic, oregano, basil, chili, and salt. Refrigerate for at least 3 hours before serving.

**THE CLASSIC**
Chopped Roma tomatoes
tossed with QCOM
Gourmet Dipping Oil

**CUCUMBER-PEPPER**
Hummus, sliced cucumber,
roasted red peppers

**CAPRESE**
Fresh mozzarella and tomato,
finished with chiffonade of basil,
pine nuts, a pinch of sea salt, and
a drizzle of extra virgin olive oil

# Pesto del Piero

MAKING PESTO IN A FOOD PROCESSOR IS QUICK AND EASY. HAND-CHOP THE INGREDIENTS IF YOU WANT A MORE RUSTIC TEXTURE.

| | |
|---|---|
| 1 | cup firmly packed fresh basil leaves |
| ½ | cup firmly packed fresh Italian parsley |
| 3 | tablespoons firmly packed fresh marjoram or oregano |
| 2 | leaves fresh sage |
| ¼ | cup roasted pine nuts or almonds |
| 2 | cloves fresh chopped garlic |
| 1 | teaspoon sea salt |
| 1 | cup extra virgin olive oil |
| ½ | cup freshly grated Parmesan cheese. |

USING A VERY SHARP KNIFE, finely chop all the fresh herbs and place them in a mixing bowl. Finely chop the nuts and garlic and add to the mixing bowl. Add salt and Parmesan cheese and mix in the olive oil.

When using the blender or food processor method, add all ingredients to the work bowl and process to desired consistency. Use a spatula to scrape down the sides. Pesto can be stored in the refrigerator for up to 10 days.

# Sweet and Hot Grilled Sausages

GRILLING THE SAUSAGES LENDS A SMOKED FLAVOR TO THIS DISH. LEMON AND FRESH OREGANO ADD A MEDITERRANEAN TWIST.

3     links hot Italian sausage

3     links sweet Italian sausage

2     tablespoons freshly chopped oregano or 1 tablespoon dried oregano

juice of 3 lemons

GRILL THE SAUSAGES until the cases are shiny and crisped. Slice and drizzle with lemon juice. Toss with oregano.

# Olive Rosettes

SIMPLE BUT LUSCIOUS FINGER FOOD.

QCOM Sun Baked Tomato Basil Stuffed Olives or other pitted and stuffed olives

sopressata salami, sliced very thin

FOLD sopressata in half lengthwise, then wrap it around the olives and secure with toothpicks. Serve as a cocktail nibble or as part of an antipasti platter.

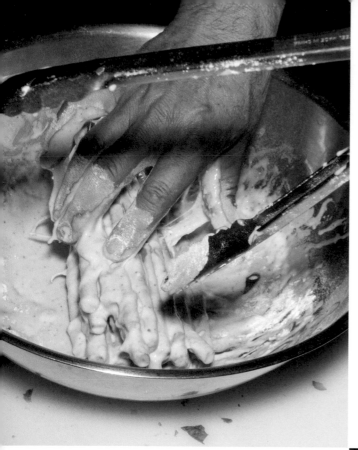

# Nonna's Asparagus Fritte

YOU MAY FIND IT ADVISABLE TO DOUBLE THIS
RECIPE, ESPECIALLY IF THE ASPARAGUS FRITTE
THIEVES ARE HANGING AROUND YOUR KITCHEN!

| | |
|---|---|
| 1 | bunch asparagus |
| 1 | cup flour |
| 2 | eggs |
| ½ | cup milk |
| 1½ | teaspoons fresh ground pepper |

oil for frying (we use a blend of 30% extra virgin
    olive oil and 70% canola oil)

sea salt

CLEAN AND TRIM the
asparagus. In a large stainless steel
or glass bowl, gently combine the
flour, eggs, milk, and pepper to
make a thick batter (it's okay if it's
slightly lumpy). Turn the asparagus
in the batter to coat.

Heat oil in a large deep frying
pan to 360°. Drop asparagus in
a few at a time. Turn them after
about 1 or 2 minutes or when their
undersides are golden brown, and
cook the other side another minute
or two. Remove to an absorbent
paper towel and sprinkle with sea
salt to taste.

26

# Caponata with Polenta and Shaved Parmesan

CAPONATA IS DELICIOUS ON TOASTED BREAD AS WELL AS POLENTA. OLIVE OIL MERGES THE RICH EGGPLANT AND PINE NUT FLAVORS WITH ACIDY TOMATO, SALTY CAPERS, AND OLIVES.

| | |
|---|---|
| 1/3 | cup extra virgin olive oil |
| 3 | cups diced eggplant |
| 2 | cups chopped onion |
| 2 | cups sliced celery |
| 1 | cup chopped green olives |
| 1/3 | cup capers, drained |
| 4 | cloves garlic, peeled and chopped |
| 1/3 | cup pine nuts |
| 2½ | cups crushed canned tomatoes |
| ¼ | cup chopped basil |
| 1 | tablespoon sea salt |
| 1 | teaspoon freshly ground black pepper |
| ½ | cup chicken broth, homemade if possible |

FOR SERVING
Creamy Polenta (page 166)
shaved Parmesan cheese
dried Sicilian-style olives

HEAT THE OIL in a large heavy skillet until it begins to shimmer. Add eggplant, onion, and celery and sauté 3 to 4 minutes, until the onions are glassy. Add the olives, capers, and garlic to the skillet and sauté another 5 minutes.

Add pine nuts, crushed tomatoes, and basil. Add the salt, pepper, and broth. Bring to a boil, then turn down the heat and simmer uncovered until the mixture has thickened, about 30 minutes. Taste and adjust seasoning.

Spoon generous servings over warm creamy polenta and garnish with Parmesan and olives. Caponata keeps in the refrigerator for up to a week

# Ricotta and Arugula Stuffed Mushrooms

BAKED STUFFED MUSHROOMS ARE A FRAGRANT PRIMI PIATTI OR COCKTAIL HORS D'OEUVRE AND MAKE A NICE ADDITION TO A BUFFET TABLE. SPICY ARUGULA IS TEMPERED BY CREAMY RICOTTA. SERVES 4.

12    baby portabella mushrooms, cleaned and stemmed
1     cup ricotta cheese
½     cup chopped arugula
1     egg, whisked
2     cloves garlic, chopped
1     teaspoon sea salt
extra virgin olive oil

ARRANGE MUSHROOMS on a baking sheet. Preheat the oven to 375°. Combine the ricotta, arugula, whisked egg, garlic, and salt in a mixing bowl. Spoon ricotta mixture into each of the mushrooms. Drizzle with olive oil and bake 8 to 10 minutes.

# Olive Tapenade del Piero

OLIVE TAPENADE HAS MANY USES IN ANTIPASTI AND OTHER DISHES. IT CAN TOP PIZZA OR FOCACCIA, BE ADDED TO A SANDWICH, OR GARNISH A PASTA DISH. BELOW IS OUR BASIC VERSION. FOR SWEET RED PEPPER TAPENADE, ADD 1/3 CUP CHOPPED ROASTED SWEET PEPPERS. MAKES ABOUT 1½ CUPS.

| | |
|---|---|
| ½ | cup pitted green olives, chopped |
| ½ | cup pitted Kalamata olives, chopped |
| 3 | tablespoons extra virgin olive oil |
| ¼ | teaspoon red chili flakes |
| 1 | clove garlic, chopped |
| ¼ | teaspoon aniseed |
| ¼ | teaspoon dried oregano |
| 1 | teaspoon balsamic vinegar |

COMBINE ALL INGREDIENTS. Cover and refrigerate for 1 hour before using. Will keep in the refrigerator for up to 7 days.

# Salami and Cheese Platter

COMPLEMENT TAPENADE AND TOASTS with an assortment of cured Italian sausages, dried figs, Castelvetrano olives, Kalamata olives, Picholine olives, Parmesan cheese, and Manchego cheese.

Pitting olives: Lay the flat side of a heavy knife on top of the olives and press down. The pits will loosen easily.

# Suppli

I FIRST TRIED THESE TASTY FRIED RICE BALLS WHEN I VISITED CEPRANO, THE TOWN MY PARENTS WERE BORN IN. ANY LEFTOVER RISOTTO WILL DO FOR SUPPLI. THE GOAL IS TO GET A CRUNCHY EXTERIOR AND CREAMY CENTER. I ALWAYS MAKE EXTRA WHEN I'M MAKING RISOTTO SO I WILL HAVE LEFTOVERS FOR THIS EASY, DELICIOUS TREAT. I LIKE TO USE PANKO (JAPANESE-STYLE DRIED BREAD CRUMBS) TO COAT THE BALLS, BUT BREAD CRUMBS WORK JUST FINE. MY FAMILY OFTEN MAKES SUPPLI FOR THE HOLIDAYS. THEY CAN BE MADE UP TO 3 HOURS AHEAD OF USE. WARM THEM IN THE OVEN BEFORE SERVING THEM WITH YOUR FAVORITE TOMATO OR MEAT SAUCE. MAKES A DOZEN OR SO.

1    tablespoon sea salt

1    cup unbleached all-purpose flour

3    eggs

1    cup panko or dry bread crumbs

2    cups risotto

12   half-inch cubes of low-moisture whole-milk mozzarella

oil for frying (we use a blend of 30% extra virgin olive oil and 70% canola oil)

COMBINE THE SALT AND FLOUR in a shallow bowl. Put the eggs in a second bowl and beat lightly. Place panko or bread crumbs in a third bowl.

Take about 2 tablespoons of cold risotto into the palm of your hand and press a cube of mozzarella into its center. Form a ball, being careful to ensure that all the cheese is hiding inside the ball. Repeat until all the risotto and cheese are used.

Dip the balls first into the flour, then the beaten egg, then the panko or bread crumbs. Press the panko or bread crumbs into the ball to form a crust. Complete all the balls and set aside on a plate.

Heat the oil to 360° in a heavy pan. You will need enough oil so that the suppli will float when frying. Fry a few balls at a time until golden brown, about 2 to 3 minutes. Place on paper towels to remove any excess oil.

# Warm Mixed Olives with Fresh Herbs

USE YOUR OWN FAVORITE COMBINATION OF NATURALLY CURED OLIVES FOR THIS DISH. MY FAVORITES ARE LISTED BELOW. SAUTÉING THEM WITH SPICES AND FRESH HERBS INTENSIFIES THEIR FLAVOR AND GIVES THEM A WONDERFUL BOUQUET.

| | |
|---|---|
| 1 | teaspoon extra virgin olive oil for sautéing, plus more for drizzling |
| 2 | cloves garlic, chopped |
| ¼ | cup Kalamata olives |
| ¼ | cup Picholine olives |
| ¼ | cup Castelvetrano olives |
| ¼ | cup Cerignola olives |
| ¼ | teaspoon ground coriander |
| 3 | sprigs chopped Italian parsley |
| 1 | teaspoon chopped fresh oregano |
| ¼ | teaspoon crushed red chili flakes |

HEAT THE OLIVE OIL in a sauté pan. Add garlic and sauté just until it begins to color. Add olives and spices. Heat throughout, about 3 minutes on medium high heat. Serve drizzled with more olive oil.

36

CURE YOUR OWN OLIVES
Use olives right off the tree that are fully purple ripe but still juicy. Manzanillo or Mission olives work well because they are the plumpest. Prick each olive with a fork a few times, then toss with rock salt. Spread the salt and olives on a cookie sheet and cover with a mesh screen to keep the bugs off. Place in a sunny spot. Turn the olives with the salt every day or so for about 7 to 10 days until they dry. (They will resemble raisins). The olives should still be moist but shriveled. Once they are cured, rinse the olives in water, let them dry completely, and pack into a mason jar. Cover with olive oil and seal. You can add any assortment of dried herbs such as oregano, aniseed, and/or red chili flakes to flavor your olives. They will keep in the refrigerator for months.

# Sizzling Manchego with Olive Tapenade

WE FIRST TASTED THIS DISH IN SPAIN'S BASQUE REGION, AND IT IMMEDIATELY BECAME A FAMILY FAVORITE. SERVES 4.

6    ounces 3-month-old Manchego cheese, rind removed
Olive Tapenade del Piero (page 33)
sliced baguette, toasted

PUT THE BLOCK of Manchego cheese in an ovenproof serving dish and place it under the broiler. Heat throughout until the cheese is bubbly and golden brown (about 5 to 6 minutes). Remove from oven and top with a dollop of olive tapenade. Serve with toasted baguette.

# Broiled Fontina-stuffed Prosciutto

THIS MAKES A GREAT ADDITION TO ANY ANTIPASTI PLATTER.

thinly sliced prosciutto
fontina cheese cut into small logs

WRAP THE CHEESE in the prosciutto and broil until the cheese is gooey and warm. Serve on whole, fresh basil leaves or on toasted sliced baguette and drizzle with extra virgin olive oil.

# Roasted Peppers

ROASTED PEPPERS ARE WORTH THE WORK, ESPECIALLY IF YOU DO A BIG BATCH AND STORE THEM COVERED IN OIL IN THE REFRIGERATOR, WHERE THEY WILL KEEP UP TO 2 WEEKS AND HAVE MANY USES. (THE OIL CAN ALSO BE USED FOR COOKING.)

**red and yellow bell peppers, poblanos, or other peppers of your choice**

WASH and dry the peppers.

GAS RANGE OR GRILL METHOD: turn the burners on high and place the peppers directly on the grates. Turn them with tongs until they're evenly charred. The peppers may hiss and bubble; it's just their moisture evaporating.

ELECTRIC RANGE METHOD: place a grill over the electric burner. Turn peppers to blacken all over.

After charring the peppers by either method, rest them in a covered bowl for about 10 minutes before peeling. The steam they release will loosen their charred skin. When the peppers are cool enough to handle but still warm, peel off the charred skin. Do not wash the peppers. Slit each lengthwise and remove the seeds and stem. Slice into strips. Turn the strips in plenty of olive oil. Roasted peppers will keep in the fridge up to about 2 weeks.

40

# Grilled Antipasti Skewers

marinated artichoke hearts, quartered
roasted red peppers
sopressata, medium sliced

SOAK six-inch wooden skewers in water. Alternately thread artichoke, red pepper and sopressata onto the skewers. Grill 2 to 3 minutes, turning as you grill. Serve hot.

# Zio Kenny's Shrimp

WE NAMED THIS DISH AFTER A GOOD FAMILY
FRIEND. IT'S ALWAYS ON THE MENU WHEN HE
VISITS!

| | |
|---|---|
| 1 | dozen jumbo shrimp, deveined and tails removed, rinsed well |
| 1 | cup cold milk |
| 4 | tablespoons extra virgin olive oil (or, for a lemony kick, 3 tablespoons olive oil and 1 tablespoon QCOM Meyer Lemon Olive Oil) |
| 1 | cup flour |
| 1 | tablespoon sea salt |
| ½ | teaspoon cayenne pepper |

FOR SAUCE TO FINISH THE DISH

| | |
|---|---|
| 1 | tablespoon butter |
| ¼ | teaspoon flour |
| 1/3 | cup freshly squeezed lemon juice |
| ¾ | cup dry white wine |

sea salt

freshly cracked black pepper

PLACE THE SHRIMP IN A BOWL with the milk and set aside. Combine the flour, salt, and cayenne pepper on a flat surface or large platter.

Heat the oil in a large, heavy-bottomed skillet over medium-high heat. When a particle of flour dropped into the oil sizzles and colors lightly, it's hot enough. The oil should not be smoking.

Remove the shrimp from the milk and dredge it in the flour mixture. Shake off the excess flour and add the shrimp to the skillet. Cook about 2 to 3 minutes per side, depending on the size of the shrimp, until crispy and golden brown. Be careful not to overcook, or the shrimp will be tough. Remove from the skillet and set aside.

Take the skillet off the heat, allow it to cool slightly (so the butter won't burn when it's added), and add butter. After it melts, add the 1/4 teaspoon flour and whisk to combine. Return the pan to low heat and add the lemon juice and wine. Boil to thicken and reduce, about 2 minutes, whisking from time to time. Add salt and pepper to taste.

Return the shrimp to the skillet so that it picks up some of the sauce. Plate the shrimp and spoon the sauce over liberally. Serve immediately, while the shrimp are still crispy.

SALAD

# Virgin Vinaigrettes

THE SIMPLEST OLIVE OIL VINAIGRETTE CAN JUST
BE A GOOD HERBACEOUS EXTRA VIRGIN OLIVE
OIL SPILLED OVER GARDEN-FRESH SALAD GREENS,
THEN DRIZZLED WITH SWEET AGED BALSAMIC
VINEGAR. THIS TRADITION IS FOLLOWED IN
KITCHENS THROUGHOUT THE MEDITERRANEAN
AND ALWAYS AT OUR DINNER TABLE. THE TYPE OF
VINEGAR YOU USE WILL DEFINE THE TARTNESS
AND SWEETNESS OF YOUR DRESSING BUT AS A
RULE OF THUMB WE USE 4 PARTS EXTRA VIRGIN
OLIVE OIL TO 1 PART VINEGAR.

### TRADITIONAL VINAIGRETTE

1    cup extra virgin olive oil
¼    cup QCOM Aged Balsamic or
     QCOM White Balsamic Vinegar
salt and pepper to taste

P U T the oil, vinegar, salt, and pepper in a mason
jar with a lid and shake to emulsify. Store in a
cool dark place. Whisk or shake again just before
drizzling. Or pour the vinaigrette ingredients into
the base of the salad bowl and whisk them together
there. Place the salad in the bowl and toss it with
the vinaigrette just before serving.

Delicious over a Mediterranean salad of
cucumber, red onion, and Roma tomatoes. Try
adding QCOM Oregano Feta-Stuffed Olives or
other olives and chopped fresh herbs.

### GARLIC VINAIGRETTE
Use QCOM Roasted Garlic Olive Oil
with white balsamic vinegar.

### BLOOD ORANGE VINAIGRETTE
Use half QCOM Blood Orange Olive
Oil and half extra virgin olive oil with
aged balsamic vinegar.

### LEMON OREGANO VINAIGRETTE
Use lemon juice instead of vinegar
and add a teaspoon of dried oregano
and a teaspoon of chopped garlic.

### STRAWBERRY OR FIG VINAIGRETTE
Use QCOM Strawberry Balsamic
Vinegar or QCOM Fig Balsamic
Vinegar instead of aged balsamic.
(Try this one over a salad of spring
mix with sliced apples, crumbled feta,
mandarin oranges, dried cranberries,
and toasted almonds.)

### POMEGRANATE VINAIGRETTE
Substitute QCOM Pomegranate White
Balsamic Vinegar.

### DIJON AND HONEY-CREAM VINAIGRETTE
Add 1 teaspoon Dijon mustard
and 2 teaspoons raw honey to the
Traditional Vinaigrette.

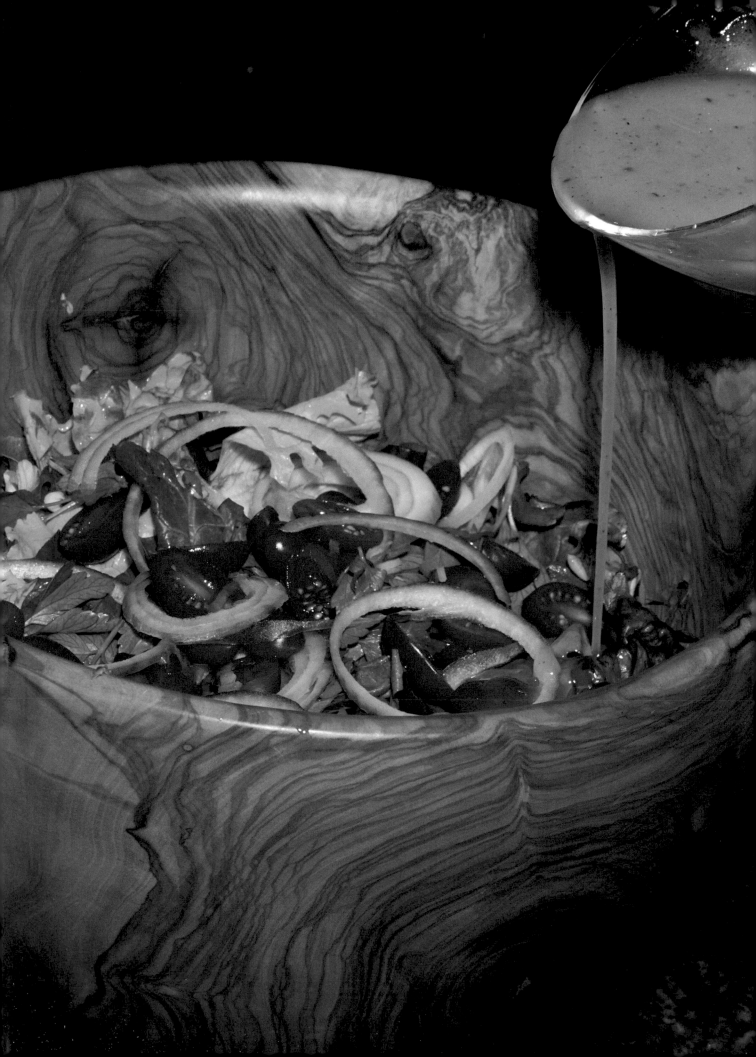

# Sonoran Spicy Green Beans

USE THE FRESHEST, SWEETEST, AND MOST TENDER GREEN BEANS YOU CAN FIND. I TURN THEM IN THE DRESSING WITH NATURE'S MOST CONVENIENT TOOL—THE HANDS. CHILI-INFUSED OLIVE OIL ADDS A SPICY NOTE AND WHITE BALSAMIC VINEGAR BRINGS A TOUCH OF ACIDY SWEETNESS. SERVES 4 TO 6.

| | |
|---|---|
| 1 | pound fresh green beans, stems removed |
| 1 | tablespoon QCOM Chili Olive Oil |
| ½ | teaspoon red chili flakes |
| ½ | teaspoon sea salt |
| 2 | tablespoons white balsamic vinegar |
| 2 | cloves garlic, peeled and sliced |

BRING 2 QUARTS OF WATER TO A BOIL. Add green beans and cook until crisp-tender. Do not overcook. Drain the beans and rinse with cold water. Put the olive oil, chili flakes, salt, and vinegar in a bowl and whisk to combine. Mix in beans and garlic. Refrigerate for 1 hour to develop flavors. The salad will keep to up to 7 days in the refrigerator.

49

# Classic Caprese

THIS IS A FAMILY FAVORITE AND EVERYBODY LOVES IT! WE USE FRESH TOMATOES AND BASIL FROM OUR GARDEN AND HAND-PULL OUR OWN FRESH MOZZARELLA (PAGE 92).

2    large vine-ripened tomatoes
fresh mozzarella
extra virgin olive oil
chiffonade of basil
QCOM Aged Balsamic Vinegar
sea salt and freshly ground black pepper

SLICE TOMATOES and fresh mozzarella. Arrange the caprese by alternating tomato and mozzarella slices. Finish with a drizzle of extra virgin olive oil and rich dark balsamic vinegar. Garnish with basil chiffonade and sprinkle with sea salt and freshly ground pepper.

# Citrus Caprese

WHEN VISITING FLORENCE, ITALY, WE CAME UPON THIS FLAVORFUL FRESH DISH. IT IS A PERFECT VARIATION OF THE CLASSIC CAPRESE FOR SHOWCASING ARIZONA'S PLENTIFUL CITRUS CROP. WE LIKE TO PICK NAVEL ORANGES RIGHT OFF THE TREE IN OUR BACK YARD.

USING A SHARP PARING KNIFE, remove the rind of the orange, leaving a thin layer of pith. When preparing this salad, use the same method as for Classic Caprese except substitute sliced oranges for the tomatoes and fresh mint for the basil.

## Chiffonade

CHIFFONADE IS A FRENCH TERM MEANING "MADE OF RAGS." IN COOKING, CHIFFONADE MEANS TO TURN INTO RAG-LIKE STRIPS. TO CHIFFONADE, STACK THE LEAVES, ROLL THEM TIGHTLY, THEN SLICE ACROSS THE LEAVES TO PRODUCE FINE RBBONS. THIS IS A NICE WAY TO SLICE HERBS LIKE MINT OR BASIL TO SCATTER OVER A DISH OR ADD TO A SALAD.

# Orange Salad with Fresh Basil

THERE ARE SO MANY SWEET ORANGES ON OUR BEAUTIFUL TREE FROM
JANUARY THROUGH MARCH THAT I AM ALWAYS LOOKING FOR EXCITING
WAYS TO SERVE THEM. THIS RECIPE IS FROM NONNA. DURING LATE MARCH
THE TREES BEGIN TO BLOOM AND THE SCENT OF ORANGE BLOSSOMS FILLS
THE VALLEY. SERVES 4.

4    medium naval oranges at room temperature
sea salt and fresh-ground black pepper
chiffonade of fresh basil
¼    cup extra virgin olive oil

USING A SHARP KNIFE, remove outer skin of the orange leaving a
light amount of pith. Do not peel. The pith will absorb the liquids in the
dish. Slice the oranges crosswise about ¼ inch thick.

　　Arrange on serving plate. Sprinkle with sea salt and fresh ground black
pepper. Garnish generously with fresh basil and drizzle with olive oil.

52

# Garbanzo Salad

MEATY, HEALTHY GARBANZOS GIVE THIS MARINATED SALAD LOTS OF BODY AND TENDER CRUNCH. QCOM WHITE BALSAMIC VINEGAR IS A GOOD CHOICE FOR ITS ACID-SWEET BALANCE. SERVES 6

2   sixteen-ounce cans organic garbanzo beans, drained and well rinsed, or approximately 4 cups home-cooked garbanzos, drained of cooking liquid

2   cloves garlic, chopped

½   cup chopped red onion

½   cup chopped celery

4   tablespoons extra virgin olive oil

4   tablespoons QCOM White Balsamic Vinegar

3   sprigs chopped Italian parsley

¼   teaspoon red chili flakes

½   teaspoon sea salt

COMBINE ALL INGREDIENTS IN A BOWL and refrigerate for 1 hour before serving so that flavors can mingle.

# ZUPPA
## PANE, PANINI

# Chicken Broth

AN AMPLE SUPPLY OF
HOMEMADE BROTH IN THE
FREEZER IS CULINARY GOLD.
WE USE GLASS JARS FOR
FREEZING BROTH, BEING
CAREFUL TO LEAVE ENOUGH
HEAD SPACE FOR THE BROTH
TO EXPAND WHEN IT FREEZES.
THIS BROTH IS THE BASE FOR
MOST OF OUR SOUP AND
RISOTTO RECIPES.

58

# Reas' Homemade Broth

HOMEMADE BROTH TASTES BETTER THAN STORE-BOUGHT AND COSTS A FRACTION OF THE PRICE, KEEPS IN THE REFRIGERATOR, FREEZES WELL, AND HAS NO ARTIFICIAL INGREDIENTS. BOTH OF THESE RECIPES MAKE 2½ QUARTS (10 CUPS). WE DON'T ADD SALT TO THE BROTH UNTIL IT IS USED IN A SOUP RECIPE.

FOR CHICKEN BROTH

| | |
|---|---|
| 3 | pound free-range chicken wings, backs, or thighs |
| 1 | tablespoon extra virgin olive oil |
| 1 | large onion, peeled and quartered |
| 3 | medium celery ribs with leaves, coarsely chopped |
| 2 | large unpeeled carrots, coarsely chopped |
| 10 | whole black peppercorns |
| 5 | sprigs Italian parsley, stems chopped off |
| 2 | bay leaves |
| 12 | cups water (or enough to cover all ingredients in pot) |

FOR BEEF BROTH

| | |
|---|---|
| 3 | pounds meaty beef bones |
| 1 | tablespoon extra virgin olive oil |
| 1 | large onion, peeled and quartered |
| 3 | medium unpeeled carrots, coarsely chopped |
| 3 | medium celery ribs, coarsely chopped |
| 10 | whole black peppercorns |
| 5 | sprigs Italian parsley, stems chopped off |
| 2 | bay leaves |
| 12 | cups water (or enough to cover all ingredients in pot) |

IN A LARGE SOUP POT heat the olive oil, then add chicken pieces or beef bones and brown slightly, about 3 to 5 minutes. Add onion, celery, carrots, black peppercorns, parsley, bay leaves, and enough water to cover the ingredients. Stir to deglaze the pot. Cover and bring to boil. Reduce heat and simmer 1½ hours. Let cool slightly.

Strain the broth into a bowl and discard the solids. Refrigerate until cold. Remove the fat from the surface. Use within 3 days if refrigerated, or keep it in the freezer for up to 6 months.

# Stracciatella

THE NAME OF THIS CLASSIC ITALIAN SOUP ("RAGS") REFERS TO THE TATTERS OF COOKED
EGG THAT LACE THEIR WAY THROUGH THE TEXTURE OF THE FINISHED SOUP. SIMPLE AND
DELICIOUS. ALL THE ITALIAN WEDDINGS I ATTENDED GROWING UP INCLUDED A SECOND
COURSE OF STRACCIATELLA. SERVES 6.

| | |
|---|---|
| 6 | cups homemade chicken broth |
| 3 | eggs |
| 3 | tablespoons grated Parmesan cheese |
| 3 | tablespoons flour |
| 1 | tablespoon Italian parsley, finely chopped |
| 1 | tablespoon lemon zest |

sea salt and freshly ground black pepper to taste

IN A LARGE STOCK POT, bring 5 cups chicken broth to a boil. In a large bowl, combine 1
cup of cold chicken broth, eggs, cheese, flour, parsley, and lemon zest. Whisk until blended.

Slowly drizzle the mixture into the boiling broth while whisking, then reduce to low heat.
Adjust seasoning with salt and pepper. Serve topped with grated Parmesan cheese.

# Roasted Butternut Squash Soup

ALONG WITH CREAMY TOMATO BASIL SOUP, ROASTED BUTTERNUT IS ONE OF THE
MOST-REQUESTED SOUPS AT DEL PIERO AT THE QUEEN CREEK OLIVE MILL. SERVES 6.

1   large butternut squash
extra virgin olive oil, about 2 tablespoons total
sea salt and freshly ground black pepper to taste
1   medium onion, chopped
4   cups homemade chicken broth
2   cups heavy cream

SPLIT SQUASH LENGTHWISE, remove all seeds and pulp, place on sheet tray, drizzle
with olive oil, and sprinkle with salt and pepper. Bake at 350° until fork tender, then set aside
to cool. When it is cool enough to handle, scrape out the flesh and discard the skin. (This step
can be done the day before.) Drizzle oil into a large soup pot, add the onion, and cook until it is
translucent. Add roasted butternut squash. Pour in enough of the broth to cover the vegetables.
Bring to a boil. Reduce heat to low, cover pot, and simmer 15 minutes. Remove from heat
and, using a stick blender, blend until smooth. Whisk in cream and heat until very hot but not
boiling.

# Zuppa Stars

WHEN OUR CHILDREN WERE BABIES, NONNA MADE HER OWN VERSION OF "ZUPPA STARS" AND BROUGHT CASES OF MASON JARS FULL OF SOUP TO STOCK OUR FREEZER. SHE MADE THE BROTH USING A WHOLE ORGANIC CHICKEN SIMMERED WITH VEGETABLES. AFTER STRAINING THE BROTH, SHE PURÉED THE BONED CHICKEN WITH THE VEGETABLES FOR ANOTHER HEALTHY HOMEMADE SOUP.

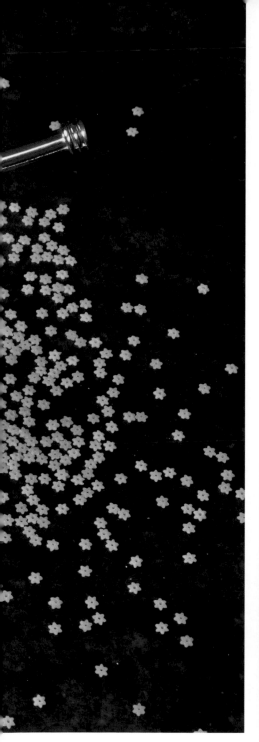

THE QUALITY OF THIS SOUP DEPENDS ON THE CARE WITH
WHICH THE BROTH IS MADE. SERVES 6.

6      cups homemade chicken broth (see page 60)
½      cup dried star-shaped pasta
Parmesan cheese
Italian parsley, chopped

A D D  1 tablespoon of salt to 4 quarts of water. Bring to a
boil and add pasta. Meanwhile, bring 6 cups of chicken broth
to boil in a soup pot. Cook "stars" to al dente, about 5 to
6 minutes. Drain and add to the hot broth. Simmer for an
additional 5 minutes. Sprinkle with grated Parmesan and
chopped parsley.

# Pasta Fagiole

THIS IS A CROSS BETWEEN A PASTA DISH AND
A HEARTY THICK SOUP. WE EAT IT WITH A BIG
SOUP SPOON (OR SOMETIMES WITH A FORK)!
SERVES 6.

¼    cup extra virgin olive oil
1     medium celery rib, chopped
1     small onion chopped
2     cloves garlic, finely chopped
¼    cup dry white wine
1     twenty-eight-ounce can whole Italian
       plum tomatoes with their juices
       (lightly chop in the blender before adding
       to the soup pot, leaving plenty of chunky
       texture)
4     cups chicken broth
2     sixteen-ounce cans cannellini beans with
       liquid, or equivalent home-cooked dried
       cannellinis

3     large sprigs chopped fresh Italian parsley
sea salt and freshly ground black pepper to
       taste
¼    teaspoon crushed red chili flakes
8     ounces spaghetti or linguini broken into
       short pieces
grated Parmesan cheese to top

PUT THE OIL IN A SOUP POT over
medium heat. Add the celery, onion, and garlic
and sauté until glassy. Add wine, tomatoes,
and broth. Stir well. Add beans, parsley, salt,
and chili flakes. Bring the soup to a boil, then
simmer 15 minutes, stirring regularly. Add
broken linguini or spaghetti.

Keep it boiling until the pasta is cooked al
dente. The soup's texture will thicken as it cooks
and the pasta absorbs the liquid. The longer it
sits the more it is like a pasta dish than a soup.

# Sausage–Escarole Soup

CHEWY AND SLIGHTLY BITTER  ESCAROLE
LEAVES BECOME SWEET AND MELLOW AS THEY
COOK, MAKING THEM PERFECT FOR SOUPS AND
STEWS. SWISS CHARD OR RAPINI ARE ALSO
GOOD CHOICES HERE. A GREAT HEARTY WINTER
SOUP THAT SHOULD BE SERVED WITH CRUSTY
ITALIAN BREAD. SERVES 6.

| | |
|---|---|
| 1 | tablespoon extra virgin olive oil |
| ¾ | pound sweet Italian sausage (left in the casing but sliced) |
| 1 | large white onion, peeled and diced |
| 2 | large carrots, peeled and diced |
| 4 | celery ribs, diced |
| 1 | sixteen-ounce can diced tomatoes (in water only, no sugar added) or 2 cups chopped tomatoes |
| 4 | cups chicken broth |
| 1 | big handful escarole, washed and chopped, tough ends removed |

sea salt and pepper to taste
dash of Tabasco, optional

HEAT THE OIL in a large stockpot and add the sausage. Brown it on both sides, about 5 minutes. Remove it from the pot with a slotted spoon and set it side.

Add onion, carrot, and celery to the pot and cook until soft, about 6 minutes. Pour in a splash of chicken broth and scrape up any browned bits of sausage. Add tomatoes and simmer.

Return the sausage to the pot. Add the remaining broth. Bring to a boil and simmer uncovered 15 minutes. Add the escarole and cook about 4 minutes longer. Season with salt, pepper, and hot sauce to taste.

73

# Meatball and Tuscan Kale Soup

BOTH FLOUR AND BREAD CRUMBS ARE USED IN THE MEATBALLS FOR THIS SOUP—FLOUR
GIVES THEM A MELT-IN-YOUR-MOUTH TEXTURE AND BREAD CRUMBS GIVE THEM BODY. THE
MEATBALLS COOK IN THE SOUP, WHICH ALSO ADDS TO THEIR MELTY QUALITY. TO KEEP THEM
TENDER, PAT THEM TOGETHER WITH THE BACK OF A SPOON JUST UNTIL THEY HOLD THEIR
SHAPE AND DON'T OVERWORK THEM. THIS HEARTY SOUP CAN BE A MEAL ON ITS OWN SERVED
WITH A WARM LOAF OF SLICED CRUSTY ARTISAN BREAD. SERVES 8.

| | |
|---|---|
| 3 | large carrots, peeled and chopped |
| 1 | small white onion, peeled and chopped |
| 1 | tablespoon extra virgin olive oil |
| ½ | pound Tuscan kale, washed and cut into bite-sized pieces |
| 10 | cups beef broth |

FOR THE MEATBALLS

| | |
|---|---|
| 1 | pound ground beef |
| ½ | small white onion, minced |
| 2 | large eggs, beaten |
| ¼ | cup plain dried bread crumbs |
| ¼ | cup all-purpose flour |
| ½ | cup freshly grated Parmesan cheese |
| | dash of freshly grated nutmeg |
| 1 | teaspoon sea salt |
| ¼ | teaspoon freshly grated pepper |

74

IN A LARGE STOCK POT, heat olive oil and add carrots, onion, and kale. Sauté 5 minutes.
Add broth and bring to boil. Reduce to simmer for 15 minutes.

Meanwhile, in a medium bowl, combine the ground beef, onion, eggs, bread crumbs, flour,
cheese, nutmeg, salt, and pepper. Mix well. Shape into walnut-size meatballs.

Carefully drop meatballs into the soup. Bring back to a soft boil and let them bubble in the
broth. Be careful not to stir too vigorously, just let them bob along. Cover and reduce heat and
simmer for ½ hour until meatballs are cooked through.

Serve with grated Parmesan cheese.

# Rea Family Multi-Grain Bread

THIS DENSE, RICHLY FLAVORED LOAF MAKES GREAT BREAKFAST TOAST (TRY IT WITH CREAMY ORGANIC PEANUT BUTTER AND HONEY) AS WELL AS SANDWICHES, AND IT'S DELICIOUS ALONGSIDE SOUP. WE ALWAYS KEEP A STASH OF MULTI-GRAIN MIX IN THE FREEZER FOR MAKING BREAD.

MAKES 2 LARGE LOAVES.

**MULTI-GRAIN MIX**
steel-cut oats
cornmeal
cracked wheat
flax seed
pumpkin seeds, toasted
sunflower seeds, toasted
cracked buckwheat, toasted
sesame seeds, toasted
millet
barley flakes

**FOR THE BREAD**
2    tablespoons active dry yeast
1     teaspoon sugar
½    cup lukewarm water
2    cups boiling water
3    cups multi-grain mix
1/3  cup molasses or honey
2    teaspoons salt
2    tablespoons sugar
1/3  cup extra virgin olive oil
1    cup cold water
2    cups whole wheat flour
2    to 3 cups bread flour

FOR THE MULTI-GRAIN MIX, combine equal parts of all or any combination of the grains and seeds listed (for example, 1 cup of each). You can mix up more than is needed for a recipe of bread and store it in the freezer for future loaves.

FOR THE BREAD, mix 1 teaspoon sugar with ½ cup lukewarm water, then add the yeast. Set aside until it's foamy, about 10 minutes.

In a separate large bowl, pour the 2 cups boiling water over the multi-grain mix. Add molasses or honey, salt, sugar, olive oil, and cold water. When cooled to lukewarm, stir in the flour and the proofed yeast mixture. Keep stirring the dough until it is well blended. Turn onto a well floured surface and knead for a few minutes.

Let rise in a covered bowl in a warm place until the dough rises to double. (Or let rise for several hours or overnight in the refrigerator. Bring to room temp before shaping.) Divide it in two and shape into loaves. Place on well greased baking sheet/ loaf pans and let rise again until double. Brush with extra virgin olive oil and using a sharp knife slit top of the loaf in the shape of a cross.

Bake at 425° for about 50 to 60 minutes. Remove from pans immediately to cool.

# Focaccia

WE USE FOCACCIA TO COMPLEMENT ANTIPASTI PLATTERS AND FOR PANINI. WHEN WE SEND THE KIDS TO SCHOOL WITH FOCACCIA IN THEIR LUNCH BOXES, THEIR SANDWICH IS THE ENVY OF THEIR FRIENDS. MAKES 2 FOCACCIA.

1     recipe Brenda's Pizza Dough (page 89)
**extra virgin olive oil**
**coarse sea salt**
**variety of toppings: fresh or dried herbs, tomatoes, olives, grated cheese, cracked black pepper**

Roll out the dough as for pizza and press it into 2 generously oiled 12- x 18-inch oblong baking sheets. Let rise 30 minutes, then prick it all over with a fork. Drizzle generously with olive oil and sprinkle with sea salt. Add toppings of your choice. Bake at 400° for 35 to 45 minutes, or until golden brown.

# Panini

PANINI ARE SIMPLY FRESH INGREDIENTS NESTLED BETWEEN FOCACCIA OR CRUSTY BREAD. THE SANDWICH IS THEN PRESSED IN A PANINI GRILL AND SERVED HOT. THE TECHNIQUE IS SIMPLE NO MATTER WHICH PANINO (A SINGLE SANDWICH) YOU MAKE. SLICE THE BREAD, BRUSH THE OUTSIDES OF THE SLICES WITH OLIVE OIL, ADD THE FILLINGS, THEN GRILL UNTIL HEATED THROUGH AND CRISPY, ABOUT 3 TO 5 MINUTES. IF YOU DON'T HAVE A PANINI PRESS, YOU CAN MAKE PANINI IN A HEAVY FRYING PAN. USE A FLAT LID WITH A DIAMETER SMALLER THAN THE DIAMETER OF THE PAN TO PRESS DOWN ON THE SANDWICH AS IT COOKS, AND FLIP ONCE SO THAT BOTH SIDES BECOME CRISP.

### SAUSAGE, PEPPER, AND OLIVE PANINI
sliced cooked sweet Italian sausage

roasted peppers

provolone cheese

sliced Kalamata olives

### CHICKEN-PESTO PANINI
sliced cooked breast of chicken

fontina cheese

pesto

sliced tomatoes

### PROSCIUTTO AND FIG PANINI
sliced prosciutto

QCOM Caramelized Red Onion and Fig Tapenade

fresh mozzarella

arugula

### ROAST BEAST PANINI
sliced roast beef

horseradish

mascarpone cheese

roasted tomatoes

### GREEN APPLE-MANCHEGO PANINI
sliced green apple

sliced manchego cheese

QCOM Sun-Dried Tomato and Parmesan Tapenade

QCOM Aged Balsamic Vinegar

### CAPRESE PANINI
sliced tomatoes

sliced fresh mozzarella

fresh basil leaves

sea salt

PIZZA

PIZZA AT OUR HOUSE IS A SALAD TO DESSERT PARTY. IT STARTS WITH MOM MAKING HER SILKY TWO-FLOUR DOUGH AND DAD HAND-PULLING FRESH WHOLE-MILK MOZZARELLA AND PROCEEDS TOWARD THE WOOD-BURNING PIZZA OVEN OUTSIDE OUR KITCHEN DOOR. FRESH SEASONAL GREENS ARE HARVESTED FROM OUR BACK YARD, DRESSED WITH ONLY OIL AND VINEGAR, AND HEAPED ON A HOT-FROM-THE-OVEN CRUST FOR THE FIRST COURSE. THEN WE EACH GET OUR OWN PERSONAL PIZZA LAYERED WITH A FAVORITE COMBINATION OF INGREDIENTS. TOPPINGS RANGE FROM TRANSLUCENT YUKON GOLDS TO CHICKEN MARSALA, WITH PESTO, A SIMPLE RICH TOMATO SAUCE, LOTS OF GOOD OLIVE OIL, AND FRESH HERBS. JUST ABOUT THE TIME YOU THINK YOU CAN'T EAT ANOTHER BITE, DAD BRINGS OUT A SIZZLING, GOOEY NUTELLA, HONEY, BANANA DESSERT PIZZA AND YOU FIND THAT—WELL—YES, YOU CAN. —JOEY REA

## Brenda's Pizza Dough

THIS DOUGH MAKES THE PERFECT PIZZA CRUST—CRISPY ON THE OUTSIDE AND SOFT AND CHEWY ON THE INSIDE. YOU CAN MAKE IT THE DAY BEFORE YOU USE IT. COVER IT WITH PLASTIC WRAP AND A TEA TOWEL, AND PLACE IT IN THE FRIDGE. NEXT DAY LET IT COME TO ROOM TEMPERATURE BEFORE SHAPING. WE LIKE KING ARTHUR UNBLEACHED ALL-PURPOSE FLOUR.

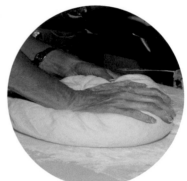

| | |
|---|---|
| 3 | cups lukewarm water |
| 1 | teaspoon sugar |
| 1 | teaspoon active dry yeast |
| 3 | to 4 cups unbleached all-purpose flour |
| 3 | to 4 cups bread flour or high-gluten pizza flour |
| 2 | tablespoons extra virgin olive oil |
| 1 | heaping tablespoon salt |

WARM THE BOWL of a stand mixer fitted with a dough hook. Pour the water directly into the bowl. Sprinkle sugar and then yeast into the water and let stand a few minutes until the yeast rises to the surface. Stir the water, sugar, and yeast together on lowest speed. Add the olive oil and stir.

Add the salt to the flour. With the mixer running, stir in the flour about a cup at a time. Continue to mix until the dough begins to form a ball, about 5 minutes. As the dough forms, it will stick to and begin to rise up the stem of the hook.

When a sticky dough has formed, scrape it out of the mixer bowl onto a well floured surface. Knead the dough for 1 to 2 minutes. Put the dough into an oiled bowl and brush the top and sides with more olive oil. Cover with plastic wrap and a tea towel. Set aside in a warm, draft-free place and allow to rise until it doubles, about 1½ to 2 hours. Punch the dough down and scrape out onto the kneading board. Form it into 8 three-inch balls. These are ready to roll out for generously sized individual pizzas.

89

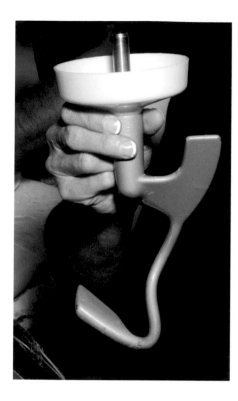

# Versatility

BESIDES THE FAMILY'S FAVORITE PIZZAS,
BRENDA'S PIZZA DOUGH IS THE BASIS
FOR CRUSTY ITALIAN SANDWICH BREAD,
FOCACCIA, ROLLS, AND THESE TREATS:

SIMPLE CINNAMON ROLLS | PAGE 185
PIZZA DOLCE | PAGE 108
PIZZA FRITTE | PAGE 190

FOR BREAD OR ROLLS, FORM THE RISEN DOUGH AND LET IT RISE A SECOND TIME BEFORE BAKING. FOR PIZZA, YOU CAN ROLL IT OUT IMMEDIATELY.

Fresh Mozzarella

**1**

92

5 pounds whole milk curd at room temperature

1/3 cup sea salt

water heated to a temperature between 150° and 165°F

**1** Cut the curd into 1-inch cubes. It's important that the cubes are all the same size so they will soften at the same rate. Place a large bowl of ice water nearby.

**2** Place the curd in another large stainless steel bowl and sprinkle with salt.

**3** Add enough of the heated water to cover the curd. Let the curd soften, about 3 minutes, stirring gently with a wooden spoon. The curds will melt together like marshmallow and become shiny.

**4** Gather the melting curd into a ball and, using your hands, fold and pull it like taffy, dipping it back into the hot water if it gets stiff. Do not overwork the curd as it will lose its butterfat.

**5** Immediately place the formed cheese into the bowl of ice water to cool.

Store in salted water for up to a week in the refrigerator.

FRESH-MADE MOZZARELLA IS SURPRISINGLY EASY AND FUN TO MAKE AT HOME. IT REQUIRES ONLY 2 INGREDIENTS AND A LITTLE PRACTICE. THE RESULT IS A FRESH CHEESE THAT IS SILKY SMOOTH, WITH A DELICATE YET RICH FLAVOR. ONE OF THE SECRETS TO A GREAT PIZZA IS FRESH-PULLED MOZZARELLA.

# Pizza Sauce

THE PIZZA SAUCE IS NOT COOKED—IT WILL COOK ON THE PIZZA WHEN IT'S FIRED IN THE OVEN.

1     twenty-eight-ounce can whole Italian plum tomatoes, drained (crush the tomatoes well in your hands as you drain the tomatoes fully)

1     clove peeled and crushed garlic

2     tablespoons extra virgin olive oil

2     teaspoons chopped fresh oregano or marjoram

sea salt to taste

PUT DRAINED TOMATOES IN THE BLENDER and puree to a smooth consistency. Place in a bowl and add the garlic, olive oil, chopped herbs, and salt. Mix well.

94

# Caramelized Onions

5   yellow or white onions, peeled and sliced
extra virgin olive oil and sea salt

HEAT THE OIL in a heavy-bottomed pan and add the onions. Turn to coat and sprinkle with salt. Cook them for about 35 to 45 minutes over medium heat, stirring occasionally. If they begin to stick to the pan, add a small amount of water to deglaze. The trick is to cook them without burning them for as long as it takes for their natural sugar to turn to deep golden caramel. Five onions will collapse to a rich 2 cups of caramelized onions. They will keep in the fridge for several days and have many uses.

# Roasted Tomatoes

12  or more ripe Roma tomatoes
extra virgin olive oil sufficient to coat the sliced
    tomatoes fully
sea salt
mixed dried Italian herbs

CUT WASHED AND DRIED Roma tomatoes lengthwise into eighths (no need to core them) and toss them with enough olive oil to coat them well.

Spread them on a baking sheet and sprinkle with salt and dried Italian herbs. Roast at 300° for 45 minutes. Remove from the oven and cool slightly, then scrape from the baking sheet, scraping in the sticky cooked juices as well as the pulp. Tomatoes will keep in the refrigerator for several days if stored in a jar and covered with extra virgin olive oil.

# Salad Pizza

any combination of your favorite
    salad greens such as
    arugula, buttercrunch, and
    red romaine
Traditional Vinaigrette (page 46)
grated Parmesan cheese
freshly ground black pepper

DRIZZLE olive oil over formed
pizza dough and sprinkle with
sea salt. Bake until golden
brown and allow to cool slightly.
Meanwhile, toss the greens with
the vinaigrette. Mound the
dressed greens atop the freshly
baked crust. Sprinkle with
Parmesan and cracked black
pepper.

## Este's Pesto Pizza

Pesto del Piero (page 23)

crumbled feta cheese

crumbled ricotta cheese

halved cherry tomatoes

marinated artichoke hearts

Mushroom Comfort (page 172)

pitted Kalamata olives

## Sydney's Chicken Marsala Pizza

truffle oil

sea salt

fontina cheese, sliced

fresh mozzarella cheese, sliced

Chicken Marsala del Piero cut in strips (page 151)

Mushroom Comfort (page 172)

Caramelized Onions (page 95)

FOR ALL THE FAVORITE COMBINATIONS, place ingredients atop a round of pizza dough in the order listed and in your preferred proportions. Then pizzas are ready to slide into a heated oven. See page 96 for pizza-baking notes.

# Joey's Yukon Gold Pizza

extra virgin olive oil

Yukon Gold potatoes, peeled
    and sliced paper thin with a mandoline

dabs of Pesto del Piero (page 23)

Caramelized Onions (page 95)

freshly chopped garlic

crumbled feta cheese

fresh mozzarella cheese, sliced

Roasted Tomatoes (page 95)

SYDNEY'S CHICKEN MARSALA PIZZA

JOEY'S YUKON GOLD PIZZA

ESTE'S PESTO PIZZA

103

# Angelo's No-Cheese Pizza

plenty of extra virgin olive oil

sea salt

freshly chopped herbs

Caramelized Onions (page 95)

halved cherry tomatoes

drizzle of Pesto del Piero (page 23)

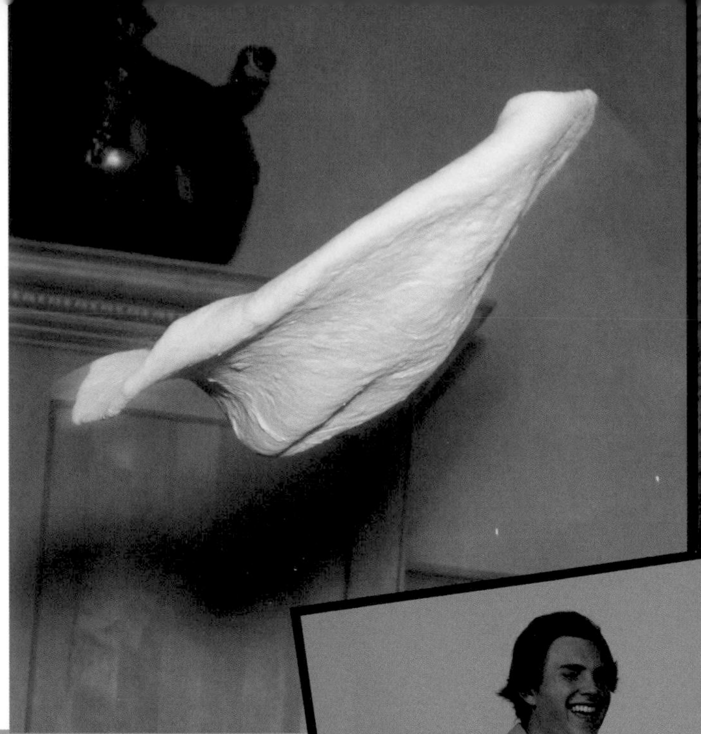

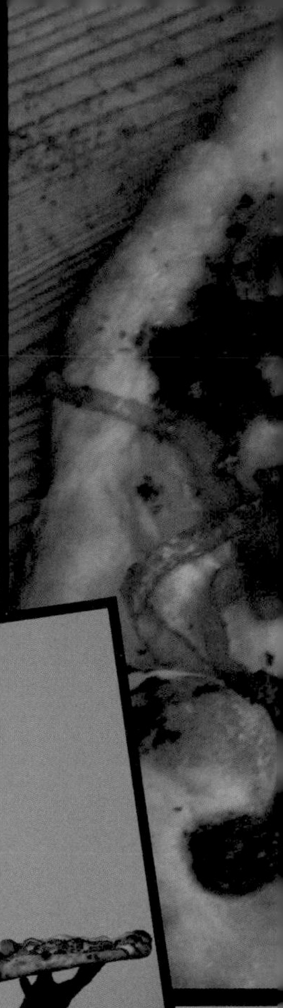

# John's Spicy Four-Pepper Pizza

Pizza Sauce (page 94)

fresh mozzarella cheese

sliced fresh green jalapeños, seeds and membranes removed

sliced fresh red jalapeños, seeds and membranes removed

small amount fresh serrano, seeds and membranes removed

slivered pickled pepperoncini

105

## Brenda's Margherita

Pizza Sauce (page 94)
fresh mozzarella cheese, sliced
fresh garden basil, added after the pizza is baked

## Pizza del Piero

Pizza Sauce (page 94)
fresh mozzarella cheese, sliced
sopressata
sweet Italian sausage
olives
mushrooms

# Pizza Dolce

THIS GOOEY, RICH CONFECTION IS IRRESISTIBLE. THE CHOCOLATE-HAZELNUT SPREAD AND MASCARPONE FORM THE "SAUCE," THE BANANAS ARE THE "PEPPERONI," AND THE HONEY IS THE "OLIVE OIL."

**butter**

**chocolate-hazelnut spread, such as Nutella**

**mascarpone cheese**

**peeled bananas, sliced into rounds**

**cinnamon**

**honey**

ROLL OUT pizza dough and shape as for pizza. Slather the round with melted butter to generously coat the whole crust. Dab with gobs of chocolate-hazelnut spread spaced evenly to mostly cover the dough. Add mascarpone by mounded tablespoons to fill in the blank spaces.

Place the sliced banana rounds on top like pepperoni. Sprinkle the pizza with cinnamon. Drizzle generously all over with honey. Bake until golden brown, so dough is just cooked but still soft and toppings are hot and melted.

# PASTA and RISOTTO

# Pappardelle with Bolognese Sauce

PAPPARDELLE IS A WIDE RIBBON PASTA. IT
MAKES FOR A HEARTY MEAL, BEST SERVED
WITH A GOOD CHIANTI. SERVES 4.

| | |
|---|---|
| 1 | pound pappardelle |
| 1 | tablespoon extra virgin olive oil |
| ½ | pound ground veal |
| ½ | pound ground pork |
| ½ | pound ground beef |
| ¼ | cup carrots, finely chopped |
| ½ | cup celery, chopped |
| 1 | small onion, chopped |
| 2 | cloves garlic, chopped |
| 1 | twelve-ounce can tomato paste |
| ½ | cup dry white wine |
| 1 | cup beef broth |
| 1 | cup heavy cream |
| 1 | teaspoon sea salt |
| 1 | rounded teaspoon freshly ground pepper |
| ¼ | teaspoon cinnamon |
| | grated Parmesan cheese |
| | sprig of parsley |

HEAT olive oil over medium-high heat in
a saucepot. Add ground veal, pork, and beef.
Sauté until lightly browned.

Add chopped carrot, celery, onions and
garlic. Cook until onions are translucent.
Mix in tomato paste, white wine and beef
broth. Bring to boil. Turn down heat and let
simmer for 10 minutes. Add heavy cream, salt,
pepper, and cinnamon. Let simmer (with lid
off) for 2 hours, stirring occasionally.

Cook pappardelle in a large pot of salted
boiling water until al dente. Drain, reserving 1
cup of the cooking water.

Toss the pappardelle with the sauce until
well combined. If it seems dry, add a bit of the
pasta cooking water. Sprinkle with Parmesan
and garnish with parsley.

# Hand-cut Savory Sausage

IN CENTRAL ITALY—IN A SMALL TOWN CALLED CEPRANO WHERE MY PARENTS GREW UP—ORANGE ZEST AND CORIANDER GIVE SAUSAGE A CHARACTERISTIC AROMA AND FLAVOR. WHEN MY DAD MAKES THIS, HE SLICES THE ORANGE SKIN AND SHREDS THE OUTER PEEL, DOING EVERYTHING BY HAND. HIS RECIPE STARTS WITH 45 POUNDS OF MEAT. HE MIXES THE SAUSAGE MEAT, PINCHES OFF A BIT AND COOKS AND TASTES IT, ADJUSTS THE SEASONINGS, TESTS IT AGAIN. "DAD," I ASKED, "WHY NOT JUST MEASURE AND DO IT THE SAME WAY EVERY TIME?" "NOT AS MUCH FUN," HE SAID. THIS ONE IS A LABOR OF LOVE. THIS SAUSAGE CAN BE USED FOR PATTIES OR RAGU.

1½ pounds pork shoulder, 80% lean

1 tablespoon finely chopped orange peel, from 1 small fresh orange (slice off the outer peel in strips, leaving behind the thickest part of the pith, and chop finely)

1 teaspoon coarse-ground coriander seeds (you can grind them in a clean coffee grinder)

1 teaspoon red chili flakes

2 teaspoons sea salt

1 teaspoon freshly ground pepper

CHOP THE PORK SHOULDER by hand to achieve a coarse-ground texture. Add the orange peel, coriander seed, red chili flakes, salt, and pepper and mix well. All seasoning should be well incorporated into the meat.

Allow the mixture to rest at least an hour or two so flavors mingle. To make patties, form the sausage meat into half-inch-thick patties. Add a small amount of extra virgin olive oil to a frying pan over medium-high heat. Brown the patties on both sides, about 4 minutes per side, until cooked through, but still juicy.

# Polenta with Hand-cut Savory Sausage Ragu

THIS IS A POOR MAN'S DINNER TRADITIONALLY SERVED TO CELEBRATE THE DECEMBER 13 FEAST OF SANTA LUCIA, PATRON SAINT OF THE IMPOVERISHED. MY MOM ALWAYS SERVES THIS IN THE TRADITIONAL STYLE, WITH THE RAGU ATOP POLENTA SPREAD ON A WOODEN BOARD.

Hand-cut Savory Sausage (page 115)

1 tablespoon extra virgin olive oil

½ cup chopped white onion

2 tablespoons dry white wine such as Sauvignon Blanc

2 twenty-eight-ounce cans good quality Italian plum tomatoes, San Marzano if possible, 1 can puréed with its liquid, the other can drained and hand-chopped

1 tablespoon chopped Italian parsley

1 clove garlic, chopped

sea salt to taste (I used about 2 teaspoons)

Parmesan cheese, grated

4 cups Basic Polenta (page 166)

HEAT A LARGE, HEAVY SAUCEPAN. Add the olive oil, onion, wine, and the sausage meat. Cook, stirring frequently, until the meat is lightly browned. Add the tomatoes, parsley, and garlic. Add salt. Bring to a boil, then reduce heat and simmer for 1 hour and 15 minutes.

To serve it the way we did at home when I was a boy, spread polenta on a large wooden board, top with the ragu, slice, and serve. The polenta firms up quickly, creating an edible platter for the ragu. Sprinkle with grated Parmesan cheese.

116

## ARCANGELO'S SAUSAGE

| | |
|---|---|
| 45 | POUNDS COARSE-GROUND OR HAND-CUT PORK, 80% LEAN |
| 1 | CUP SEA SALT |
| 1 | CUP CORIANDER (FRESH GROUND) |
| 8 | ORANGE RINDS, FINELY CHOPPED |
| 3 | OUNCES FRESH GROUND PEPPER |
| 3 | OUNCES RED CHILI FLAKES |

MIX WELL AND LET SIT OVER NIGHT IN THE REFRIGERATOR. PLACE IN CASINGS
USING A SAUSAGE STUFFER. HANG IN A COOLER FOR 2 TO 3 DAYS, THEN FREEZE.

# Fettuccine wtih Burnt Butter Mizithra, Spinach and Kalamata Olives

WE USE AN AGED MIZITHRA CHEESE WHICH IS QUITE AROMATIC. THE SHREDDED CHEESE DOES NOT MELT IN THE BUTTER AND RETAINS ITS SHAPE AFTER COOKING. SERVES 4.

| | |
|---|---|
| 1 | cup chopped fresh spinach |
| | drizzle of extra virgin olive oil |
| | sea salt |
| 1 | cup finely shredded mizithra cheese |
| ½ | cup unsalted butter |
| 1 | pound fettuccine, cooked in salted water al dente and drained (reserve 1 cup cooking water) |
| ¼ | cup pitted Kalamata olives |

HEAT OLIVE OIL in a medium skillet and add spinach and salt. Cook until the spinach is wilted, about 1 to 2 minutes. Remove with a slotted spoon, chop, drain, and set aside. Add the butter to the still warm pan the spinach was cooked in. Add a drizzle of olive oil to keep the butter from burning. Butter will melt and foam slightly.

Stir in the shredded mizithra and cook until amber in color, about 2 to 3 minutes. The mizithra will pop, giving off a pleasantly nutty caramel aroma. Stir in the spinach and olives and combine with the cooked fettucine.

Add some of the reserved pasta cooking water if the dish is too dry. Add salt to taste; mizithra is a salty cheese, so more salt may not be necessary.

# Farfalle with Sun-dried Tomatoes, Olives and Creamy Pesto

THIS RICH PESTO-BASED PASTA DISH IS BEST SERVED WITH A GLASS OF CHILLED PINOT GRIGIO. SERVES 4.

| | |
|---|---|
| 1 | pound farfalle pasta |
| 3 | tablespoons Pesto del Piero (page 23) |
| ¼ | cup sun-dried tomatoes, chopped |
| 1/3 | cup olives, pitted and halved |
| 1 | cup chicken broth |
| ½ | cup heavy cream |
| ¼ | cup Parmesan cheese, grated |

COOK PASTA in salted water until al dente. In a skillet, combine pesto, sun-dried tomatoes, olives and chicken broth. Bring to a boil, then remove from heat. Stir in cream. Salt to taste. Add pasta and toss. If the dish is too dry, add some of the reserved pasta cooking water. Place in a serving dish and sprinkle with grated Parmesan cheese.

# Simply Red Sugo

THE SIMPLEST TOMATO SAUCES CONSIST OF JUST
CHOPPED RED-RIPE PLUM TOMATO FLESH COOKED
IN A LITTLE EXTRA VIRGIN OLIVE OIL AND SIMMERED
UNTIL IT LOSES ITS RAW FLAVOR, THEN SEASONED
WITH SALT, FRESH HERBS, ONION, AND GARLIC. USE
THIS NATURALLY BALANCED RED SAUCE ("SUGO") AS IS
OR AS A BASE TO CREATE YOUR OWN SIGNATURE RED
SAUCE. ANGELO'S FAVORITE! SERVES 4.

| | |
|---|---|
| ¼ | cup extra virgin olive oil |
| 1 | small onion, diced |
| 1 | 28-ounce can whole peeled San Marzano tomatoes (do not drain) |
| 1 | 6-ounce can tomato paste |
| 4 | cloves garlic, chopped |
| ¼ | cup chopped fresh basil |
| 1 | teaspoon sea salt |
| ½ | teaspoon freshly ground pepper |
| ¼ | cup Chianti |

HEAT A SAUCEPAN over medium-high heat and
add olive oil and onion. Cook until the onions are glassy,
about 4 to 5 minutes.

Add the tomatoes and paste and bring to a boil.
Lower heat and simmer for 20 minutes.

With a stick blender, blend all ingredients to a
smooth consistency. (Or transfer to a blender and blend
in batches, return to saucepan). Bring to simmer again
and add garlic, basil, salt, pepper, and wine. Continue to
simmer for about 20 more minutes.
Toss the Sugo with cooked spaghetti and top with your
favorite additions.

**PASTA TOPPINGS**

SOME OF OUR FAVORITES, SHOWN
AT LEFT, CLOCKWISE FROM TOP:

• SHAVED PARMESAN CHEESE
• ROASTED EGGPLANT
• PAN-SAUTÉED MUSHROOMS AND
GRILLED SAUSAGES
• SAUTÉED PEPPERS AND ONIONS
WITH FRESH HERBS

# Peppery Limoncello Linguine

THE SWEETNESS OF LIMONCELLO ACTS TO TEMPER THE SPICY CHILI OIL AND TART
LEMON FLAVORS IN THIS LINGUINE DISH. OFTEN REQUESTED AND ALWAYS A HIT
IN OUR HOME! SERVES 4.

1    pound linguine

½    cup QCOM Chili Oil

juice and zest from half a lemon

1    ounce limoncello

3    tablespoons toasted pine nuts

½    cup feta cheese, crumbled

¼    to ½ teaspoon red chili flakes

2    to 3 sprigs Italian parsley, chopped

COOK PASTA in a large pot of boiling salted water until al dente. While pasta is
cooking, whisk together the chili oil, lemon juice, lemon zest, and limoncello. Drain
the cooked pasta, reserving 1 cup of pasta cooking water. Add the hot pasta to the
chili oil mixture.

Add the crumbled feta, pine nuts, red chili flakes. Toss. Season generously with
salt and pepper. If pasta is too dry, add some of the reserved pasta cooking water.
Serve sprinkled with chopped parsley.

# Gemelli with Chicken in Fontina Cream Sauce

BE CAREFUL NOT TO OVERCOOK THE CHICKEN IN THE BEGINNING HERE, SINCE IT IS GOING TO COOK LONGER AND YOU WANT TO KEEP IT TENDER. A CREAM-BASED PASTA CAN BECOME TOO THICK EVEN IN THE TIME IT TAKES TO MOVE IT TO THE TABLE. TO MAKE IT SILKY AGAIN, ADD A BIT OF PASTA COOKING WATER. SERVES 4.

- 3 tablespoons extra virgin olive oil
- 1 tablespoon minced shallot
- 3 organic chicken breast halves cut into half-inch strips
- 1 tablespoon minced garlic
- 1/2 cup sun-dried or roasted tomatoes, chopped
- 3/4 cup medium dry white wine
- 3 cups heavy cream
- 4 ounces fontina cheese, grated
- sea salt to taste
- 3 sprigs Italian parsley, chopped
- 1 pound gemelli pasta
- chopped parsley and fresh marjoram leaves to garnish

HEAT OLIVE OIL IN A SAUTÉ PAN. Add shallot and chicken and sauté 8 to 10 minutes. Add garlic and tomatoes and cook 1 minute. Add wine and cook until the mixture is reduced by half. Add cream, bring to a light boil, then simmer and reduce again by a third. Stir in fontina cheese until melted.

Cook pasta in a large pot of salted boiling water until al dente. Drain, reserving 1 cup of the cooking water.

Pour cream sauce over pasta and toss. If pasta is too dry, moisten with some reserved cooking water from the pasta. Garnish with chopped herbs.

# Not Your Mangia-Cake's Mac 'n' Cheese

"MANGIA-CAKE" IS A TERM USED LOVINGLY BY ITALIANS FOR NON-ITALIANS. THIS IS THE ITALIAN VERSION OF THE VERY MANGIA-CAKE MAC 'N CHEESE. SERVES 4 TO 6.

| | |
|---|---|
| 1 | pound rigatoni |
| ½ | pound fontina cheese, grated |
| ½ | pound aged white cheddar cheese, grated |
| 2 | tablespoons extra virgin olive oil |
| 2 | cloves garlic, peeled and chopped |
| 1 | large sprig fresh thyme |
| 1 | large sprig fresh rosemary |
| 1 | large sprig fresh sage |
| ½ | cup dry white wine |
| 2 | tablespoons flour |
| 4 | cups whole milk |
| 2 | tablespoons Dijon mustard |
| ¼ | teaspoon cayenne pepper |
| sea salt and cracked black pepper | |
| ¼ | cup coarse dry bread crumbs |
| ¼ | cup grated Parmesan cheese |

COOK THE PASTA in a large pot of salted boiling water until not quite al dente. The pasta needs to be underdone so that it will absorb the sauce. Drain and immediately rinse under cold running water to stop the cooking, then drain again and set aside.

Grate the fontina and cheddar with a box grater and set aside.

Put the olive oil in a large saucepan over medium heat. Add the garlic and fresh herbs. Cook until the garlic is soft and beginning to change color but not browned, 3 to 4 minutes, stirring constantly. Add the wine. Stir to deglaze the pan, about 2 to 3 minutes. Remove the solids, pressing with the back of a spoon to release their flavors. It's OK to leave bits behind.

Pour in the milk and whisk to combine. Immediately add the flour (add it while the milk is still cold so that it will not clump) and whisk until smooth.

Cook over medium heat about 8 to 12 minutes, until the mixture thickens, stirring frequently. Set aside 1 cup of the grated cheese and add the rest a handful at a time, stirring to melt. When the cheese is all melted, whisk in the Dijon mustard and the cayenne. Add salt and pepper to taste.

Stir the rigatoni into the sauce completely so the tubes are fully coated and the sauce goes inside them. Transfer to an 8- to 9-cup baking dish. Top with the reserved cup of grated cheese, the Parmesan, and the bread crumbs.

Bake about 25 minutes at 400°. Let rest 5 to 10 minutes and serve.

VARIATIONS: Add any combination of broccoli florets, sliced red pepper, cooked chicken, or asparagus when assembling the dish before baking.

131

# Spaghetti with Shrimp and Oil-Cured Black Olives

I USE THE OIL-CURED BLACK OLIVES MADE BY MY DAD FOR THIS DISH. YOU CAN FIND OIL-CURED BLACK OLIVES IN THE DELI SECTIONS OF GOURMET FOOD STORES. SAN MARZANO TOMATOES ARE THE MOST FLAVORFUL BUT OTHER GOOD QUALITY PLUM TOMATOES WILL ALSO WORK. AS THE FRESH HERB SPRIGS SAUTÉ, YOU WILL BEGIN TO SMELL THEIR STEMMY, EARTHY AROMA.

4   tablespoons extra virgin olive oil

2   tablespoons chopped white onion

1   large sprig each of rosemary, marjoram, sage

2   cloves garlic, minced

1   twenty-eight-ounce can peeled plum tomatoes with their liquid (half left whole, half crushed very lightly in a food processor or blender)

3   cups organic or homemade chicken broth (page 60)

1   cup dry white wine

pinch red chili flakes

freshly cracked black pepper

30  oil-cured black olives, not pitted

1   pound extra large raw shrimp, shelled and deveined

1   pound spaghetti

PUT THE OLIVE OIL IN A medium-sized heavy-bottomed soup pot. Add the onion and herbs and cook until the onion is glassy. Remove the herbs. Add the garlic and sauté 2 minutes or until soft, being careful not to brown. Add the tomatoes, broth, wine, and red chili flakes and bring to a soft boil. Reduce to simmer and add shrimp and olives. Simmer 10 to 15 minutes, crushing the whole tomatoes from time to time with the back of a spoon.

Meanwhile cook the spaghetti in salted boiling water until al dente, drain and add to soup pot and combine. Serve hot with a spoon and a fork—this is a very soupy dish, and the broth is delicious. Serve with fresh crusty Italian bread to sop up any leftover broth in your bowl.

133

# Risotto

SLOW-COOKED ARBORIO RICE TURNS CREAMY
AND SUBSTANTIAL WHEN COOKED RISOTTO-
STYLE. THE QUALITY OF THE BROTH—
HOMEMADE IS BEST—AND THE DRY WHITE
WINE ARE KEY (MAKE SURE TO HAVE PLENTY
FOR SIPPING WHILE YOU STIR). BEYOND THAT,
IMAGINATION IS KING: TRY VARIOUS FAVORITE
HERBS, CHEESES, AND OTHER INGREDIENTS.

# Risotto with Crisp-Tender Vegetables

THIS IS BRENDA'S ABSOLUTE FAVORITE RISOTTO. IF MADE WITH VEGETABLE BROTH,
IT IS A VEGETARIAN DISH. SERVES 4.

136

| 3 | tablespoons extra virgin olive oil |
|---|---|
| ½ | cup chopped onion |
| 1 | cup arborio rice |
| ½ | cup dry white wine |
| 20 | ounces hot chicken or vegetable broth |
| | plus 2 ounces for later |
| 2 | tablespoons mascarpone cheese |
| ½ | cup Fontina cheese, grated |
| 2/3 | cup asparagus, chopped |
| 2/3 | cup tricolor peppers, chopped |
| ½ | cup zucchini, chopped |
| ¼ | cup carrot, julienned |
| ½ | cup broccoli florets, chopped |
| ½ | cup Parmesan cheese, grated |
| 1 | teaspoon sea salt or to taste |

freshly ground black pepper to taste

HEAT OLIVE OIL in a 4-quart saucepan on medium-high heat. Add onion and sauté until translucent, about 5 minutes. Mix in the rice and cook for 1 minute. Add wine and stir until the wine is absorbed into the rice. Add broth one ladleful at a time and stir after each addition until broth is absorbed. Rice should be al dente.

Fold in Parmesan, mascarpone, and Fontina cheeses until they melt. Add all the vegetables and the remaining broth and mix well. Add salt and pepper and cook covered 5 minutes on low heat. Serve with extra grated Parmesan cheese.

# Wild Mushroom Risotto

IF YOU LIKE TO SIP WINE WHILE COOKING, RISOTTO IS FOR YOU. THERE'S PLENTY OF TIME TO ENJOY A NICE GLASS WITH YOUR FRIENDS WHILE YOU GENTLY TEND THE RISOTTO. SERVES 4.

| | |
|---|---|
| 1 | tablespoons extra virgin olive oil |
| 2 | tablespoons QCOM Truffle Olive Oil plus extra to finish |
| ½ | cup chopped onion |
| 1 | cup arborio rice |
| 2 | cups fresh sliced mushrooms of your choice |
| 1 | cup dry white wine |
| 20 | ounces hot chicken broth |
| ½ | cup mascarpone cheese |
| 1 | teaspoon sea salt or to taste |

freshly ground pepper to taste

HEAT OLIVE OIL AND TRUFFLE OIL in a 4-quart sauce pan on medium-high heat. Add chopped onion and sauté until translucent, about 5 minutes. Mix in 1 cup rice and cook 1 minute. Add mushrooms and wine and stir until wine is absorbed into rice. Add chicken broth one ladleful at a time, stirring between additions until the broth is absorbed. Rice should be al dente. Melt in Mascarpone cheese. Salt and pepper to taste. Serve finished with truffle oil.

PIATTI
MEAT, FISH, EGGS

# Tilapia Cepranese

THE DELICATE WHITE MEAT OF TILAPIA PAIRS WITH A CRISPY
PANKO CRUST TO MAKE THIS A FAVORITE OF MY WIFE
BRENDA. SEA BASS, GROUPER, CATFISH, OR RED SNAPPER CAN
BE SUBSTITUTED FOR THE TILAPIA. SERVES 4.

| | |
|---|---|
| 4 | six-ounce tilapia fillets |
| 1½ | cups cold milk |
| 1 | cup all-purpose flour |
| ½ | teaspoon sea salt |
| ½ | teaspoon freshly ground pepper |
| 3 | large eggs |
| 1 | cup Panko bread crumbs |
| 1/3 | cup chopped fresh parsley |

finely grated zest of ½ lemon (about 2 teaspoons)

lemon wedges for serving

| | |
|---|---|
| 6 | to 7 tablespoons extra virgin olive oil |
| 4 | tablespoons unsalted butter |
| 6 | cups baby arugula or mixed seasonal greens |

PREHEAT OVEN TO 425°. Soak fillets in cold milk.
Meanwhile mix the flour with ½ teaspoon each of salt and
pepper in a shallow bowl. Lightly beat the eggs in another
shallow bowl. Combine the breadcrumbs, parsley, and lemon
zest in a third shallow bowl.

One at a time, remove the fillets
from the milk and dredge them in
the flour, shaking off the excess. Dip
them in the egg mixture, then coat
them with the breadcrumbs, gently
pressing to coat both sides. Transfer
to a large plate.

Line a baking sheet with foil.
Heat 2 tablespoons each of extra
virgin olive oil and butter in large
skillet over medium-high heat. Add
2 fillets at a time and cook until
golden about 3 minutes per side.
Transfer to the baking sheet. Repeat
with the remaining 2 fillets adding
2 more tablespoons of olive oil and
butter. Transfer the fish to the oven
and bake until cooked through
about 7 to 8 minutes.

Toss the arugula with the
remaining 2 to 3 tablespoons of
extra virgin olive oil. Salt and
pepper to taste. Serve the fish with
salad and garnish with lemon
wedges.

143

# Almond Mustard-Crusted Salmon Fillets

HERE TANGY DIJON AND WHOLE-GRAIN MUSTARD BALANCE THE RICH SALMON FLAVOR, AND ALMONDS CREATE A CRISPY CRUST. THIS IS ANGELO'S FAVORITE FISH DISH. LEFTOVERS DISAPPEAR WHEN HE ROLLS INTO THE KITCHEN AFTER SCHOOL OR HITTING THE GYM. SERVES 6.

| | |
|---|---|
| 3 | garlic cloves, minced |
| 3 | tablespoons crushed raw almonds |
| 2 | tablespoons Dijon mustard |
| 2 | tablespoons whole-grain mustard |
| 1 | teaspoon finely chopped fresh thyme |
| 3/4 | teaspoon finely chopped fresh rosemary |
| 1 | tablespoon dry white wine |
| 1 | tablespoon extra virgin olive oil plus more to coat the baking dish |
| 6 | six- to eight-ounce salmon fillets |
| sea salt and freshly ground pepper | |
| 6 | lemon wedges |

MIX the garlic, almonds, both mustards, thyme, rosemary, wine and olive oil in a small bowl. Set the paste aside.

Preheat the broiler. Line a heavy rimmed baking sheet with foil and coat with olive oil. Arrange the salmon fillets skin side down on the baking sheet and sprinkle with salt and pepper. Broil on high for 3 minutes. Remove from the oven and spread the almond mustard paste evenly over each fillet. Continue broiling until the fillets are just cooked through and golden brown about 5 more minutes. Transfer to plates and serve with lemon wedges.

# Lemon Chicken del Piero

THIS LIGHT LEMONY CHICKEN DISH CAN BE MADE IN LESS THAN 30 MINUTES. THE "SECRET INGREDIENT" IS THE FRESHLY SQUEEZED LEMON JUICE. SERVES 4.

| | |
|---|---|
| 2 | skinless, boneless chicken breasts |
| ½ | cup unbleached all-purpose flour for dredging |
| 1 | tablespoon sea salt |
| 1 | teaspoon freshly ground pepper |
| | dash of cayenne pepper |
| ¼ | cup extra virgin olive oil |
| 2 | tablespoons unsalted butter |
| ½ | cup dry white wine |
| ½ | cup chicken broth |
| 1 | clove garlic, minced |
| 2 | lemons, 1 juiced and 1 thinly sliced for garnish |
| ¼ | cup capers |
| 4 | sprigs Italian flat leaf parsley, chopped |

BUTTERFLY CHICKEN BREASTS, MAKING 4 CUTLETS. Combine flour, salt, pepper and cayenne pepper in a shallow bowl. Dredge the chicken cutlets in the seasoned flour mixture and set aside. Heat the oil over medium high heat in a large skillet.

Sauté the chicken cutlets for about 3 to 5 minutes each side until golden, turning once. (Do in batches if the cutlets do not fit in the pan.) Set cutlets aside in a single layer and keep warm.

Add the lemon juice, chicken broth, capers, garlic, and wine, scraping down the bits from the pan for extra flavor, and bring to boil. Let simmer and whisk in butter. Return chicken to pan to warm it. Season with salt. Arrange chicken on platter and pour sauce over chicken. Garnish with parsley and lemon sauce.

## Dredging

DREDGING IS A PROCESS IN WHICH FOODS ARE PULLED THROUGH DRY INGREDIENTS IN ORDER TO COAT THEM BEFORE COOKING. FLOUR CAN BE USED ALONE OR COMBINED WITH HERBS, SPICES, SALT, OR BREADCRUMBS.

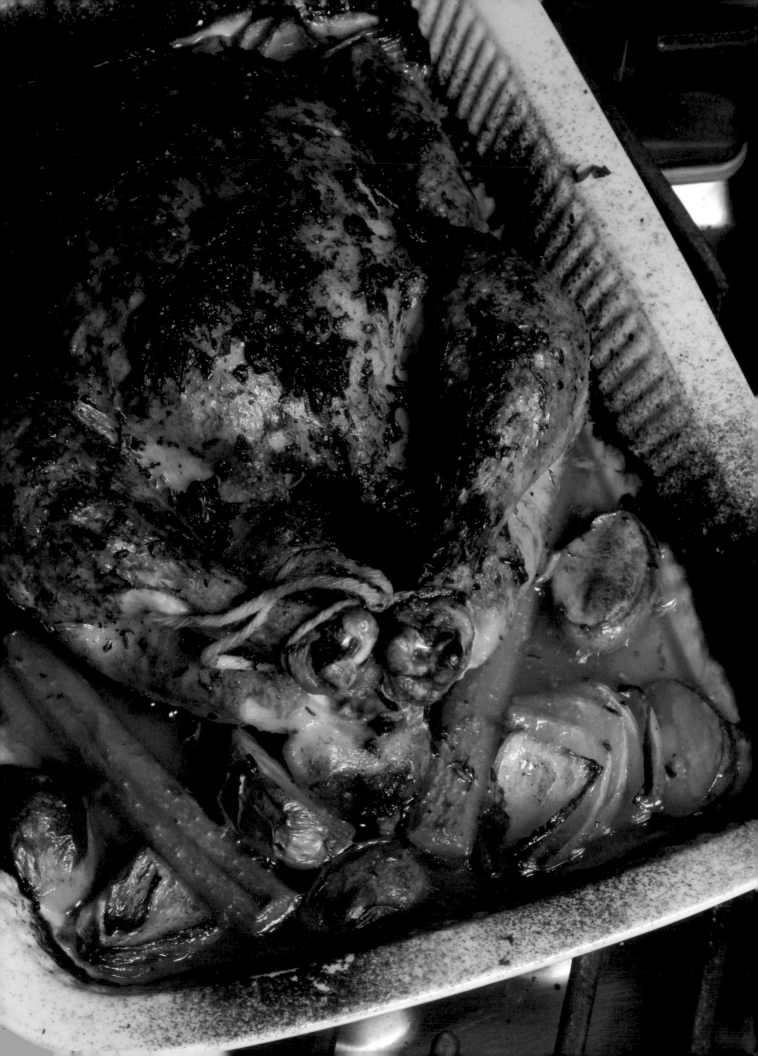

# Fresh Herb-Crusted Roast Chicken

I AM ALWAYS LOOKING FOR SOMETHING TO DO WITH THE BOUNTY OF FRESH HERBS IN MY GARDEN. HERE I CREATED AN HERB PASTE TO COAT THE CHICKEN BEFORE ROASTING. COOKING THE CHICKEN WHOLE ENSURES THAT THE MEAT WILL BE TENDER AND MOIST. WE SERVE THIS WITH THE FLAVORFUL ROASTED VEGETABLES AND PAN-SAUTÉED GREENS. SERVES 4 TO 6.

1    free range chicken, about 4 to 5 pounds

juice of ½ lemon

½    cup extra virgin olive oil

1    tablespoon sea salt

½    teaspoon fresh ground pepper

sprig of fresh rosemary

1    medium onion, peeled and quartered

2    celery ribs, quartered

6    small potatoes peeled

3    medium whole carrots, peeled

¼    cup chopped fresh rosemary

¼    cup chopped Italian parsley

5    leaves sage, chopped

¼    cup chopped thyme

¼    cup chardonnay

½    cup chicken broth

PREHEAT OVEN TO 350°. In a mixing bowl, combine the lemon juice, olive oil, salt, pepper, and chopped herbs. Mix well to form a light paste. Rub the outside and inside of the chicken with the herb paste, reserving about 1 tablespoon. Insert the rosemary sprig into the cavity of the chicken. Toss the onion, celery, potatoes, carrots, wine, and chicken broth with the reserved tablespoon of herb paste. Place the chicken in a shallow roasting pan. Nestle the vegetables around the chicken and pour any remaining liquid into the roasting pan, being careful not to disturb the herb-coated chicken. Roast for about 20 minutes per pound. Baste several times during cooking. When the chicken is done, internal temperature should register about 170° on a meat thermometer inserted into the meaty part of the thigh.

Transfer the chicken to a serving dish and surround it with the roasted vegetables.

# Chicken Marsala

MUSHROOMS AND MARSALA ARE MY
KIND OF "M & M"S. MARSALA IS ITALY'S
VERSION OF FORTIFIED WINE. WHILE OFTEN
RECOGNIZED MORE FOR ITS USE IN THE
KITCHEN, IT IS ALSO A GOOD SIPPING WINE,
LIKE PORT OR SHERRY. SERVES 4.

2   skinless, boneless chicken breasts
½   cup all-purpose flour for dredging
1   tablespoon sea salt
1   teaspoon freshly ground pepper
¼   cup extra virgin olive oil
8   ounces crimini or porcini mushrooms,
    sliced ¼ inch thick
½   cup Marsala wine
½   cup chicken broth
2   tablespoons unsalted butter
4   sprigs Italian flat leaf parsley, chopped

BUTTERFLY CHICKEN BREASTS, making 4 cutlets. Combine flour, salt and pepper in a shallow bowl. Dredge the chicken cutlets in the seasoned flour mixture shaking to remove excess flour. Heat the oil over medium high heat in a large skillet. Sauté the chicken cutlets for about 3 to 5 minutes each side until golden brown, turning once.

Set cutlets aside in a single layer and keep warm. Turn heat to medium high, add mushrooms, and sauté until they are nicely browned, about 5 minutes. Pour the Marsala wine in the pan and boil down for a few seconds to evaporate the alcohol. Add the chicken broth, simmering for a minute or so until sauce is reduced slightly. Stir in butter and season with salt and pepper. Return chicken to pan.

Heat the chicken through, about 2 minutes. Plate the chicken and top with mushrooms and sauce. Garnish with chopped parsley.

# Grilled Lamb Chops with Lemon-Mint Sauce

THIS DISH WAS INSPIRED BY BRENDA'S
GRANNY, IVY, WHO WOULDN'T EAT PASTA
BUT ABSOLUTELY LOVED LAMB. THE BRIGHTLY
FLAVORED LEMON-MINT SAUCE SERVES AS
BOTH MARINADE AND DRIZZLING SAUCE. IF
YOU WIND UP WITH EXTRA, IT'S GREAT ON
SHRIMP OR CHICKEN AS WELL. SERVES 4 TO 6.

12 lamb chops, four to five ounces each

FOR THE SAUCE

1    cup extra virgin olive oil

juice of 2 lemons (about ½ cup)

½    cup fresh chopped mint

½    cup fresh chopped Italian parsley

½    cup thinly sliced green onions

¼    cup capers, drained and chopped

2    teaspoons grated lemon zest

1    small fresh Serrano pepper, ribs removed,
     chopped

3    cloves garlic, chopped

3½   teaspoons sea salt

1½   teaspoons freshly ground pepper

STIR THE OIL, LEMON JUICE, mint,
parsley, green onions, capers, lemon zest
and serrano pepper together in a large bowl.
Whisk in 1½ teaspoons of salt and ½ teaspoon
ground pepper. Set the sauce aside.

Place the lamb chops in a large glass baking
dish. Rub the remaining salt, black pepper and
garlic all over the chops. Pour ½ cup of the
sauce over the chops, turning to coat evenly.
Reserve the remaining sauce.

Prepare a charcoal or gas grill for medium
high heat. Grill the lamb chops on each side
about 4 minutes per side for medium rare.
Remove from grill.

Arrange the lamb chops on a platter and
drizzle with some of the reserved sauce. Serve
the remaining sauce as a condiment alongside
the lamb. Nice with a side of Rosemary
Roasted Potatoes (page 163).

152

# Chocolate Fig Balsamic Steak with Radicchio

THE COMBINATION OF OUR QCOM CHOCOLATE OLIVE OIL AND SWEET FIG BALSAMIC VINEGAR GIVES THE SAUCE A RICH FLAVOR THAT WORKS PERFECTLY WITH JUICY STEAK. FLANK STEAK IS A LEAN CUT AND SHOULD BE SERVED MEDIUM RARE AT MOST. SERVES 4.

| | |
|---|---|
| 1 | two-pound flank or flat iron steak |
| | sea salt and freshly ground pepper |
| 3 | tablespoons QCOM Chocolate Olive Oil |
| 2 | tablespoons sugar |
| 1 | clove garlic, chopped |
| 2 | heads radicchio, chopped |
| 1 | teaspoon white wine |
| 1/3 | cup sun-dried tomatoes thinly sliced |
| ¼ | cup QCOM Fig Balsamic Vinegar |
| 1 | cup chicken broth (page 60) |
| ¼ | cup basil, chiffonade |
| 1 | tablespoon chopped parsley |
| | shaved dark chocolate |

HEAT A LARGE SKILLET over medium high to high heat. Season the steak generously with salt and pepper. When the pan is very hot add chocolate olive oil, swirling the pan to coat. Cook the steak to desired doneness. About 8 minutes per side for medium rare. Transfer to a cutting board.

Reduce the heat to medium and add 1 tablespoon of butter to the skillet. Add the garlic and cook until the garlic floats to the top, about 30 seconds. Add the radicchio in batches tossing until wilted. Add 1 teaspoon white wine. Sprinkle with ½ teaspoon of salt. Add the sun-dried tomatoes and fig balsamic vinegar and cook until the vinegar evaporates slightly, about 1 minute. Add the broth and cook until the radicchio is tender about 2 minutes. Stir in the basil. Remove the radicchio and set aside. Stir in the remaining tablespoon of butter and continue to cook until sauce thickens, about 2 minutes. Thinly slice the steak across the grain and place on a serving platter. Arrange radicchio around the meat and drizzle with the sauce. Garnish with parsley and shaved dark chocolate.

# Spinach-and-Ricotta Stuffed Chicken Pillows in Fresh Tomato-Herb Sauce

THIS DISH IS A WONDERFUL BALANCE OF DELICATE RICOTTA, FRESH TOMATOES AND HERBS, WITH A HINT OF NUTMEG. SERVES 4.

| | |
|---|---|
| 4 | boneless, skinless chicken breasts |
| ¼ | cup water |
| 2 | cups spinach, firmly packed |
| 2 | cloves garlic, chopped |
| 1 | teaspoon sea salt |
| 1 | cup whole milk ricotta cheese |
| ½ | cup grated Pecorino Romano cheese, |
| 1 | whole beaten egg |
| ¼ | teaspoon freshly grated nutmeg |
| 3 | tablespoons extra virgin olive oil |

large plastic food storage bags or waxed paper and toothpicks for assembling

FRESH TOMATO-HERB SAUCE

| | |
|---|---|
| 1 | tablespoon extra virgin olive oil |
| 1 | clove garlic chopped |
| 1 | twenty-eight-ounce can chopped tomatoes |
| 5 | tablespoons chopped basil leaves |
| 4 | tablespoons chopped parsley |

sea salt and freshly ground pepper

PLACE CHICKEN BREASTS in a plastic food bag or between two large sheets of wax paper. Pound out the chicken from the center of the bag outward using a mallet or heavy bottom skillet. The breasts should end up about double the size of the original breast.

Add water to a medium sized skillet and bring to a boil. Add spinach and cook until wilted. Remove from heat, drain well and chop. Set aside.

FOR THE SAUCE: In a medium sized sauce pan heat 2 tablespoons olive oil. Add chopped garlic and cook for about 1 minute. Add the chopped tomatoes and bring to a simmer. Add chopped basil and parsley. Add salt and pepper to taste. Continue to simmer.

FOR THE STUFFING: In a bowl combine chopped spinach, garlic, salt, ricotta cheese, Pecorino Romano cheese, egg, and nutmeg.

TO ASSEMBLE: Place a quarter of the stuffing on each breast and wrap breast over the stuffing. Secure breasts with toothpicks. Heat 3 tablespoons olive oil in a large non-stick skillet. Add breasts to the pan and brown all sides about 12 to 15 minutes. Remove breasts and add sauce to the skillet. Carefully remove the toothpicks from the chicken breasts and return to the pan. Reduce heat, cover, and simmer 5 minutes. Serve the chicken breasts with generous spoonfuls of the sauce.

# Asparagus and Summer Squash Frittata

THIS IS A WONDERFUL, HEALTHY, EASY-TO-PREPARE BREAKFAST OR ANYTIME MEAL. FOLLOW THE GENERAL METHOD USING YOUR FAVORITE VEGETABLES AND CREATE YOUR OWN FRITTATA. LEFTOVERS CAN BE SANDWICHED BETWEEN TWO SLICES OF CRUSTY ITALIAN BREAD. SERVES 4.

| | |
|---|---|
| 8 | eggs |
| 1/3 | cup milk |
| 2 | sprigs Italian parsley, chopped |
| ½ | teaspoon sea salt |
| | sprinkle of freshly ground black pepper |
| 3 | tablespoons extra virgin olive oil |
| 1/3 | cup chopped green onions |
| 1/3 | cup chopped zucchini |
| 1/3 | cup chopped asparagus |
| 1/3 | cup chopped yellow squash |
| 1/3 | cup grated Parmesan cheese, firmly packed |

WHISK EGGS, MILK, CHEESE, parsley, salt, and pepper together in large bowl. Heat the olive oil in a 10-inch nonstick skillet over medium heat. Add onions, zucchini, asparagus, and yellow squash to pan and sauté until glassy, about 4 minutes. Add a pinch of salt. Pour the egg mixture into the skillet. Let cook at medium-low heat for 10 to 12 minutes. When the center is almost set, place the skillet in a heated broiler to finish cooking and lightly brown the top.

Loosen the frittata with a spatula and slide it onto a serving plate. Delicious with Rosemary Roasted Potatoes (page 163).

# Rosemary Roasted Potatoes

THIS IS SO SIMPLE, YET SO DELICIOUS, IT'S BOUND TO BECOME A FAMILY FAVORITE. YOU CAN GIVE IT A GREEK TWIST BY SUBSTITUTING QCOM MEYER LEMON OLIVE OIL. SERVES 6.

12 or so mini new potatoes or 4 medium larger new potatoes

3 tablespoons extra virgin olive oil

2 tablespoons fresh rosemary, chopped

sea salt and black pepper to taste

3 sprigs fresh Italian parsley, chopped

sprig fresh rosemary to garnish

PREHEAT OVEN TO 400°. Scrub new potatoes and cut them in half (in eighths, if the potatoes are large). In a large bowl, combine the olive oil with the rosemary, salt, pepper, and parsley. Add potatoes and mix well to cover.

Spread on a large baking sheet skin side down in a single layer. Roast on the middle rack of the oven for approximately 35 to 40 minutes or until the potatoes are golden. Do not turn potatoes while roasting. Remove from the oven and salt again if you wish. Garnish with rosemary.

# Polenta Four Ways

FROM HUMBLE ORIGINS, POLENTA NOW APPEARS ON THE FANCIEST RESTAURANT MENUS, USUALLY SERVED TOPPED WITH ANY NUMBER OF SAUCES. IT HAS BECOME A FAVORITE ACCOMPANIMENT OF MANY DISHES AT OUR DINNER TABLE AND CAN BE USED AS A GLUTEN FREE ALTERNATIVE TO PASTA. POLENTA IS ALSO AN EXCELLENT SOURCE OF IRON AND VITAMIN B6.

INFUSED EXTRA VIRGIN OLIVE OIL CAN REPLACE THE BUTTER IN THIS RECIPE. I LIKE TO ADD 3 TABLESPOONS OF WHITE TRUFFLE OIL INSTEAD OF BUTTER TO CREATE AN EARTHY TASTING CREAMY POLENTA. SERVES 6.

### BASIC POLENTA

| | |
|---|---|
| 6½ | cups water |
| 2 | teaspoons sea salt |
| 13/4 | cups yellow cornmeal |
| 3 | tablespoons unsalted butter |

BOIL THE WATER in a large heavy saucepan. Add the salt. Keeping the water at a rolling boil, whisk in the cornmeal slowly until the cornmeal is completely blended in and there are no lumps. Reduce the heat to low and cook, stirring often, until the mixture thickens and the cornmeal is tender, about 15 to 20 minutes. Remove from heat. Add the butter and stir until melted.

### BAKED POLENTA

Start with the basic polenta recipe and cook as described. Turn the polenta onto a board and spread with a knife to ½ inch thick. Let cool. Use a sharp knife dipped in hot water to cut the polenta into squares. Grease a shallow pan with extra virgin olive oil and arrange squares of the cooled polenta in a single layer. Brush top of polenta with extra virgin olive oil. Bake at 350° for 30 minutes until a crispy top layer forms. Serve sprinkled with grated Parmesan cheese. Or serve as a bed for your favorite stew or grilled vegetables.

### CREAMY POLENTA

Start with the basic polenta recipe and cook as described. Take 3 cups of the basic polenta and add ½ cup of heavy cream. Stir together and bring to a simmer in a heavy saucepan. Serve creamy polenta topped with Mushroom Comfort del Piero (page 172) or Savory Sausage Ragu (page 116).

### GRILLED POLENTA

Start with the basic polenta recipe and cook as described. Turn the polenta onto a board and spread with a knife to 1/4 inch thick. Let cool. Use a sharp knife dipped in hot water to cut the polenta into squares. Brush with extra virgin olive oil and grill on a BBQ or in a gridded stovetop skillet, leaving pronounced grill marks. Serve with Garlic Sautéed Swiss Chard (page 168), Lemon Chicken del Piero (page 146), or topped with your favorite light salad.

# Sautéed Radicchio with Sun-dried Tomatoes

SERVES 4 TO 6.

1    tablespoon butter

1    tablespoon extra virgin olive oil

1    clove garlic, chopped

2    heads radicchio, chopped

1    tablespoon white wine

1/3  cup sun-dried tomatoes, thinly sliced

¼    cup QCOM Fig Balsamic vinegar

¼    cup chicken broth

**sea salt to taste**

HEAT BUTTER AND OIL in a sauté pan over medium-high heat. Add the garlic and cook until the garlic floats to the top, about 1 minute. Add the radicchio and wine and cook until wilted. Add the sun-dried tomatoes and fig balsamic vinegar and cook until the vinegar evaporates slightly, about 2 minutes. Add the broth and cook until the radicchio is tender, about 2 minutes more. Salt to taste.

# Cinnamon Glazed Carrots

CARAMELIZED CARROTS DEVELOP A SWEET NATURAL GLAZE. A DELICIOUS SIDE FOR MEAT OR FISH ALONG WITH ROASTED GARLIC MASHED POTATOES (PAGE 164). SERVES 6.

5    medium carrots, peeled and sliced, or use 1 pound ready-to-eat peeled baby carrots

1    tablespoon QCOM Vanilla Bean Olive Oil

¼    teaspoon ground cinnamon

1    cup chicken broth (page 60)

3    tablespoons brown sugar

SAUTÉ THE CARROTS IN OLIVE OIL for 2 minutes. Add cinnamon, chicken broth, and brown sugar. Cook until the liquids are absorbed and carrots are tender.

# Mushroom Comfort del Piero

VERSATILE MUSHROOM COMFORT CAN BE SERVED WARM AS A SIDE DISH OR COLD AS A SALAD. GREAT WITH STEAK OR ATOP A TOASTED SLICE OF BAGUETTE. MAKES 2 1/2 CUPS.

| | |
|---|---|
| 1 | pound mushrooms (button, cremini, or portabello or a mix), sliced |
| ¼ | cup chopped onion |
| 4 | tablespoons extra virgin olive oil |
| 1 | ounce Southern Comfort whiskey |
| 4 | tablespoons low-sodium soy sauce |
| 1 | tablespoon chopped fresh rosemary |
| 2 | tablespoon chopped garlic |

dash of red chili flakes

SAUTÉ THE MUSHROOMS AND ONIONS IN OLIVE OIL for 3 minutes. Add the Southern Comfort and fire the pan to evaporate the alcohol. Add soy sauce, rosemary, garlic, and chili flakes and sauté for 3 more minutes.

DESSERT

CREAM CHEESE VARIATION

MAKE CREAM CHEESE FILLING TO
PUT BETWEEN THE LAYERS: MIX
8 OUNCES CREAM CHEESE WITH
1 CUP SUGAR AND 1 TEASPOON
VANILLA. FOLD IN 1 CUP WHIPPED
CREAM.

# Double Chocolate Olive Oil Cake

THIS CAKE IS A FAMILY FAVORITE AND HOLDS
A SPECIAL PLACE IN OUR HEARTS. NOT ONLY
WAS IT OUR WEDDING CAKE IN 1987, BUT
IT HAS MADE AN APPEARANCE AT EVERY
BIRTHDAY SINCE—AND THAT MEANS 7 TIMES
A YEAR!

178

## FOR THE CAKE

| | |
|---|---|
| 1¾ | cups all-purpose flour |
| 2 | cups sugar |
| ¾ | cup sifted cocoa powder |
| 1½ | teaspoons baking powder |
| 1½ | teaspoons baking soda |
| 1 | teaspoon salt |
| 2 | eggs |
| 2 | teaspoons vanilla |
| ½ | cup QCOM Chocolate Olive Oil |
| 1 | cup milk |
| 1 | cup boiling water |

## FOR THE FROSTING

| | |
|---|---|
| 1½ | cups butter at room temperature |
| 3 | cups powdered sugar |
| 2 | cups cocoa powder |
| 6 | tablespoons hot coffee or espresso |
| 6 | tablespoons milk |
| 2 | teaspoons vanilla |

FOR THE CAKE, butter two 9-inch round
cake pans and preheat the oven to 350°.
In a large bowl, blend the flour, sugar, cocoa,
baking powder, baking soda, and salt. Mix in
the eggs, vanilla, and chocolate olive oil. Add
the milk and beat on medium speed until
fairly well mixed. Add the boiling water as
soon as the milk is mixed in. Continue to beat
at low speed or by hand. The mixture should
be runny but uniform. Divide between the
2 cake pans (each should be about 2/3 full)
and bake 40 minutes on the middle rack. The
cake is done when a toothpick inserted in the
center comes out clean. Do not open the oven
door while the cake is baking. Cool in pans
10 minutes, then remove to wire racks to cool
completely.

FOR THE FROSTING, combine the butter, powdered sugar and cocoa in a food processor, pulsing a few times to blend. Leave it a little chunky, almost like pastry dough. Add the hot coffee, milk, and vanilla and blend again to mix, stopping to scrape down the sides as needed. If it is a little too thin, add a bit more powdered sugar.

TO ASSEMBLE: Using a serrated knife, slice each layer in half horizontally to create 4 layers. Put the first layer on a cake stand and frost the top of the layer. Add the second layer and frost its top. Repeat for the third layer. Stack the final layer and frost the sides of the cake, then the top of the cake. Decorate as desired.

179

# Cannoli

CANNOLI ARE A DELICATE AND SIMPLE-TO-ASSEMBLE DESSERT. FOR BEST RESULTS, USE A GOOD QUALITY WHOLE MILK RICOTTA. MAKES 24 MINI CANNOLI.

2   cups whole milk ricotta cheese
3   tablespoons powdered sugar
½   teaspoon cinnamon
½   cup heavy cream, whipped stiff
3   to 4 tablespoons mini semi-sweet chocolate bits (optional)
24  pre-made cannoli shells

BEAT RICOTTA CHEESE with powdered sugar and cinnamon. Fold in the cream and chocolate chips. Pipe the filling into the shells, and finish by dipping the ends of the cannoli in crushed pistachios, crushed hazelnuts, or mini semi-sweet chocolate chips.

# Healthy Chocolate Chip Cookies

THESE FREEZE WELL AND ACTUALLY TASTE GOOD WHEN EATEN FROZEN! MAKES ABOUT 4 DOZEN.

½    cup butter (whole stick), softened
½    cup QCOM Vanilla Bean Olive Oil
1¼   cup brown sugar, firmly packed
2    eggs
1    cup unbleached all-purpose flour
1    cup whole wheat flour
¼    cup whole ground flaxseed meal
1    teaspoon baking soda
½    teaspoon salt
2    cups steel-cut oats
1½   cups any combination of chocolate chips/chopped walnuts/raisins

PREHEAT OVEN to 350°. Beat butter, olive oil, and brown sugar until creamy. Add eggs and beat well. In a separate bowl, combine the flours, flaxseed meal, baking soda, and salt. Add the dry mixture to the oil mixture. Mix in oats and chocolate chips/chopped walnuts/raisins until combined.

Drop dough by tablespoon onto an ungreased cookie sheet.

Bake 8 to 10 minutes or until golden brown. Cool for 1 minute and then remove to wire rack to finish cooling.

# Double Chocolate Biscotti

MAKES 28.

| 1 | tablespoon QCOM Chocolate Olive Oil |
| 1 | stick butter, softened |
| 1 | cup sugar |
| 4 | eggs |
| ½ | teaspoon vanilla extract |
| 2 | cups unbleached all-purpose flour |
| ½ | cup cocoa powder |
| 1 | tablespoon baking powder |
| ½ | cup chocolate chips |
| ¾ | cup whole hazelnuts or blanched almonds (optional) |

IN A MIXING BOWL, cream the oil, butter, and sugar. Add eggs, one at a time, beating well after each. Stir in the vanilla extract. In a separate bowl, combine the flour, cocoa powder, and baking powder. Add to the creamed mixture. Mix in chocolate chips and nuts. Cover and chill for 1 to 2 hours.

Preheat the oven to 375°. Line a baking sheet with parchment paper. Divide dough in half and spread into two 12- x 3-inch rectangles on parchment. Use the back of a large spoon dipped in water to shape dough and smooth top. Bake 15 to 20 minutes or until firm to the touch. Remove from oven and reduce heat to 300°. Allow to cool 15 minutes. Place the rectangles on a cutting board and using a serrated knife, slice diagonally half an inch thick. Place slices cut side down on ungreased baking sheet. Bake 10 minutes. Turn biscotti over and bake 10 minutes more. Turn the oven off, leaving biscotti in the oven with the door ajar to cool.

# Almond Biscotti

MAKES 28.

| ½ | cup QCOM Vanilla Bean Olive Oil |
| 1½ | cups sugar |
| 4 | eggs |
| ½ | teaspoon almond extract |
| 2½ | cups unbleached all-purpose flour |
| 3 | cups almond meal (see tip, page 196) |
| 4 | teaspoons baking powder |
| ¼ | teaspoon sea salt |
| ¾ | cup whole blanched almonds |

PREHEAT OVEN TO 375°. In a mixing bowl, cream the olive oil and sugar. Add eggs, one at a time, beating well after each addition. Stir in almond extract. In a separate bowl, combine the flour, almond meal, baking powder, and salt. Add to creamed mixture. Mix in whole blanched almonds.

Line a baking sheet with parchment paper. Divide dough in half and spread into two 12-inch x 3-inch rectangles on parchment. Use back of a large spoon dipped in water to shape dough and smooth top. Bake 15 to 20 minutes or until golden brown and firm to the touch. Remove from oven and reduce heat to 300°. Allow to cool for 15 minutes.

Place the rectangles on a cutting board and using a serrated knife slice diagonally ½ inch thick. Place slices cut side down on ungreased baking sheet. Bake 10 minutes. Turn biscotti over and bake 10 minutes more. Turn the oven off, leaving biscotti in oven with door ajar to cool.

# Simple Cinnamon Rolls

THIS IS ONE OF OUR YUMMIEST USES FOR
LEFTOVER PIZZA DOUGH. IT CAN BE KEPT
IN THE REFRIGERATOR OVERNIGHT, THEN
BROUGHT TO ROOM TEMPERATURE BEFORE
ROLLING OUT IN THE MORNING.

1    recipe Brenda's Pizza Dough
     (page 89)
½   cup melted butter
½   cup brown sugar
cinnamon

POWDERED SUGAR GLAZE
½   cup powdered sugar
1    teaspoon milk

186

ROLL OUT a piece of dough to about
½ inch thick into the shape of a rectangle.
Using a pastry brush, slather on melted
butter to cover dough. Layer on a heavy
sprinkling of brown sugar and then a
sprinkling of cinnamon to cover melted
butter. Roll up dough, starting with the wide
edge of the rectangle, into a tube. Cut 1 inch
thick pieces and place cut-side down on a
well buttered baking pan.

    Cover with plastic wrap and a tea towel
and let rise for about 30 minutes. Bake at
350° for 20 to 25 minutes. Turn immediately
on to a cooling rack.

    For the glaze, mix the powdered sugar
and milk, adding a few more drops of milk if
necessary to achieve a drizzling consistency.
Drizzle on warm cinnamon buns. Serve
warm.

# Cinnamon Swirl Coffeecake

## FOR THE TOPPING

1/3   cup brown sugar, packed

¼   cup flour

1   teaspoon cinnamon

¼   cup butter, cold

## FOR THE COFFEECAKE

1   eight-ounce package cream cheese, softened

1   cup sugar

½   cup butter, softened

2   eggs

1   teaspoon vanilla

1¾   cup unbleached all-purpose flour

1   teaspoon baking powder

½   teaspoon baking soda

¼   teaspoon salt

¼   cup milk

188

PREHEAT the oven to 350°.

FOR THE TOPPING: Combine brown sugar, flour, and cinnamon. Cut in cold butter until mixture resembles coarse crumbs.

FOR THE COFFEECAKE: In a mixing bowl combine cream cheese, butter and sugar until well-blended. Add eggs and vanilla and mix well. In a separate bowl combine flour, baking powder, baking soda and salt. Add to cream cheese mixture alternately with milk.

Pour batter into greased and floured 13- x 9-inch baking pan. Sprinkle with topping and swirl knife through batter to mix in topping.

Bake 30 minutes or until a wooden toothpick inserted into the center of the cake comes out clean. Cool in the pan.

# Pizza Fritte

EVERY CHRISTMAS EVE, NONNA AND PAPA BRING OVER A HUGE BASKETFUL OF FRESHLY
MADE PIZZA FRITTE. IT NEVER MAKES IT TO THE DESSERT TABLE!

Brenda's Pizza Dough (page 89)
extra virgin olive oil and and canola oil combined for frying
powdered sugar
cinnamon

ADD ENOUGH OLIVE OIL and canola oil to a deep frying pan so that it reaches ½ inch
deep (use ¾ canola oil and ¼ olive oil). Heat oils to 360 -370°.
Stretch golf ball-size pieces of the dough to any shape you want. Fry in oil until golden brown,
turning once.

Drain on paper towels. Sprinkle with powdered sugar and cinnamon while warm.

# Blood Orange Olive Oil Cupcakes

MAKES 18.

3 eggs
1 cup QCOM Blood Orange Olive Oil
1 tablespoon orange juice
1¼ cups milk
2 cups sugar
1 teaspoon salt
2 cups unbleached all-purpose flour
1 teaspoon baking powder
½ teaspoon baking soda

ORANGE FROSTING

½ cup butter (room temperature)
4 cups powdered sugar
3 tablespoons orange juice
¼ cup heavy cream
optional: a few drops of orange food coloring

194

PREHEAT the oven to 325°. Whisk together the eggs, olive oil, orange juice, and milk. In a separate bowl combine the sugar, salt, flour, baking powder, and baking soda with a whisk. Mix the wet ingredients with the dry ingredients and stir until smooth. Pour into cupcake cups and bake 25 to 30 minutes. Cupcakes are done when a toothpick inserted in the center comes out clean.

Beat the frosting ingredients together in a mixer until smooth and creamy and spread on the cooled cupcakes.

# Vanilla Bean Olive Oil Cupcakes

MAKES 18.

3 eggs
1 cup QCOM Vanilla Bean Olive Oil
1¼ cups milk
2 cups sugar
1 teaspoon salt
2 cups unbleached all-purpose flour
1 teaspoon baking powder
½ teaspoon baking soda

VANILLA FROSTING

½ cup butter (room temperature)
4 cups powdered sugar
1 teaspoon vanilla extract
½ cup heavy cream

PREHEAT the oven to 325°. Whisk together the eggs, olive oil, and milk. In a separate bowl combine the sugar, salt, flour, baking powder, and baking soda with a whisk. Mix the wet ingredients with the dry ingredients and stir until smooth. Pour into cupcake cups and bake 25 to 30 minutes. Cupcakes are done when a toothpick inserted in the center comes out clean.

Beat the frosting ingredients together in a mixer until smooth and creamy and spread on the cooled cupcakes.

# Chocolate Olive Oil Cupcakes

MAKES APPROXIMATELY 2 DOZEN.

1¾ cups all-purpose flour

2 cups sugar

¾ cup sifted cocoa powder

1½ teaspoons baking powder

1½ teaspoons baking soda

1 teaspoon salt

2 eggs

2 teaspoons vanilla

½ cup QCOM Chocolate Olive Oil

1 cup milk

1 cup boiling water

CHOCOLATE FROSTING

1½ cups butter at room temperature

3 cups powdered sugar

2 cups cocoa powder

6 tablespoons hot coffee or espresso

6 tablespoons milk

2 teaspoons vanilla

PREHEAT the oven to 325°. In a mixer, blend the flour, sugar, cocoa, baking powder, baking soda, and salt. Mix in the eggs, vanilla, and chocolate olive oil. Add the milk and beat to blend. Add the boiling water. Continue to beat at low speed. The batter will be thin. Pour into cupcake cups and bake 20 to 25 minutes. Cupcakes are done when a toothpick inserted in the center comes out clean. Cool in pan for 10 minutes then remove to wire rack to cool completely.

Beat the frosting ingredients together in a mixer until smooth and creamy. Spread on cooled cupcakes.

# Mexican Lime Olive Oil Cupcakes

MAKES 18.

3 eggs

1 cup QCOM Lime Olive Oil

1 tablespoon lime juice

1¼ cups milk

2 cups sugar

1 teaspoon salt

2 cups unbleached all-purpose flour

1 teaspoon baking powder

½ teaspoon baking soda

LIME FROSTING

½ cup butter (room temperature)

4 cups powdered sugar

3 tablespoons lime juice

¼ cup heavy cream

optional: a few drops of green food coloring

PREHEAT the oven to 325°. Whisk together the eggs, olive oil, lime juice, and milk. In a separate bowl combine the sugar, salt, flour, baking powder, and baking soda with a whisk. Mix the wet ingredients with the dry ingredients and stir until smooth. Pour into cupcake cups and bake for 25 to 30 minutes. Cupcakes are done when a toothpick inserted in the center comes out clean.

Beat the frosting ingredients together in a mixer until smooth and creamy and spread on the cooled cupcakes.

195

# Meyer Lemon Olive Oil Cupcakes

MAKES 18.

3   eggs
1   cup QCOM Meyer Lemon Olive Oil
1   tablespoon lemon juice
1¼  cups milk
2   cups sugar
1   teaspoon salt
2   cups unbleached all-purpose flour
1   teaspoon baking powder
½   teaspoon baking soda
½   teaspoon lemon zest

LEMON FROSTING
½   cup butter (room temperature)
4   cups powdered sugar
3   tablespoons lemon juice
¼   cup heavy cream
optional: a few drops of yellow food coloring

PREHEAT the oven to 325°. Whisk together the eggs, olive oil, lemon juice, and milk. In a separate bowl combine sugar, salt, flour, baking powder, baking soda and lemon zest. Mix the wet ingredients with the dry ingredients and stir until smooth. Pour into cupcake cups and bake 25 to 30 minutes at 325°. Cupcakes are done when a toothpick inserted in the center comes out clean.

Beat the frosting ingredients together in a mixer until smooth and creamy and spread on the cooled cupcakes.

# Ricciarelli Cookies

MAKES 1 DOZEN COOKIES.

1   egg white
2   teaspoons amaretto liqueur
¼   teaspoon almond extract
2   cups almond meal (see below)
1   cup powdered sugar (extra for dusting)
½   teaspoon baking powder
15  whole almonds, optional

PREHEAT OVEN TO 350°. Line a baking sheet with parchment paper. Lightly whisk egg white. Add liqueur and almond extract and whisk again.

In a separate bowl, mix the almond meal with the powdered sugar and baking powder. Make a well in the middle, add the egg white mixture, and stir to make a stiff dough. Divide the dough into 12 pieces and roll each into a ball. Place them on the baking sheet. Press an almond lightly into the center of each ball.

Bake 12 to 15 minutes until cookies are golden brown. Dust with powdered sugar. Leave on baking sheets to cool for a few minutes, then transfer to wire racks to cool completely.

## Almond Meal

TO MAKE YOUR OWN ALMOND MEAL, GRIND WHOLE BLANCHED ALMONDS TO A FINE POWDER IN A NUT GRINDER OR A FOOD PROCESSOR.

# Peanut Butter Balls

HOLIDAYS AT OUR HOUSE ARE NEVER WITHOUT THIS MELT-IN-YOUR MOUTH TREAT (WE JUST HAVE TO KEEP THEM AWAY FROM JOHN!) MAKES ABOUT 6 DOZEN.

1½   cups smooth peanut butter

¼     cup butter, softened

2     cups powdered sugar

1     teaspoon vanilla

2     cups semi-sweet chocolate chips or chopped dark chocolate

IN A MIXING BOWL, combine peanut butter, butter, powdered sugar, and vanilla. Mix until smooth. Scoop a tablespoonful of peanut butter mixture into your hand and shape into a ball. Set on a baking sheet covered in waxed paper. Continue until all mixture is used. Refrigerate 30 minutes.

In the meantime, melt chocolate chips in a heavy saucepan on low heat, stirring constantly so as not to burn the chocolate. Using tongs, dip balls into melted chocolate to cover and set on baking pan covered in wax paper. Refrigerate until chocolate is set.

# Brownies Bellisimo

1   cup butter, softened

4   one-ounce squares unsweetened chocolate

2   cups sugar

1   teaspoon vanilla

3   eggs

1   cup unbleached all-purpose flour

½   teaspoon salt

1½  cups chocolate chips

PREHEAT oven to 350°. Melt ½ cup of the butter with chocolate over low heat; cool. Cream the remaining butter, sugar, and vanilla in separate bowl. Add eggs one at a time beating after each addition. Stir in cooled butter and chocolate mixture.

Add flour and salt. Mix until well blended.

Pour into a greased and floured 13- x 9-inch pan. Sprinkle chocolate chips over surface. Bake at 350° for 30 minutes. Cool in pan.

# Praline Cheesecake

FOR THE BASE

| | |
|---|---|
| 1 | heaping cup graham cracker crumbs |
| 1/3 | cup melted butter |
| ¼ | cup crushed pecans |
| ¼ | cup sugar |

FOR THE FILLING

| | |
|---|---|
| 1½ | pounds cream cheese (3 eight-ounce packages) |
| 1 | cup brown sugar, packed |
| 3 | eggs |
| 2 | teaspoons vanilla |
| 1 | cup heavy whipping cream |

FOR THE TOPPING

| | |
|---|---|
| 1/3 | cup butter |
| 2/3 | cup brown sugar |
| ¼ | cup crushed pecans |

PREHEAT oven to 450°. Cut a piece of cardboard that will fit into the bottom of a 9-inch springform pan and cover it with aluminum foil. Place in the bottom of pan.

FOR THE BASE: Mix together the base ingredients and pour them into the prepared springform pan. Pat out evenly with the back of a spoon.

FOR THE FILLING: Break up the cream cheese into a food processor and add the sugar. Blend until all lumps are gone. Add the eggs and vanilla and mix well. Add the whipping cream while the processor is running. Pour the filling into the prepared springform pan over the base.

BAKE THE CHEESECAKE: Bake at 450° for 10 minutes, then turn oven down to 250° and continue baking 1½ hours. Check after 1 hour and 20 minutes. It's done when it is uniformly stiff to the touch but still has a slight jiggle. Run a sharp knife around edge immediately after removing from oven.

When cooled, transfer cake to serving plate, leaving it atop the cardboard.

FOR THE TOPPING: Heat the butter in a saucepan. When it is almost melted, add the brown sugar and stir until smooth. Pour topping on the completely cooled cake and spread to the sides. Let it run over the sides a little. Smooth the topping surface by rubbing it with the back of a spoon heated under hot running water. Sprinkle crushed pecans around perimeter of cake. Refrigerate well before serving.

# Vanilla Bean Waffles

JOHN LOVES HIS CHOCOLATE CHIP WAFFLES. JUST ADD CHOCOLATE CHIPS AFTER ALL OTHER INGREDIENTS. SERVE WITH A SCOOP OF ICE CREAM AND DRIZZLE WITH CHOCOLATE SAUCE. THIS WAFFLE RECIPE IS ALSO GREAT AS A BREAKFAST WAFFLE WITH PURE MAPLE SYRUP DRIZZLED OVER THE TOP. ADD YOUR FAVORITE BERRIES AND/OR VANILLA YOGURT FOR A VARIATION.

| | |
|---|---|
| 2 | eggs |
| 1½ | cups buttermilk |
| ½ | cup QCOM Vanilla Bean Olive Oil |
| 2 | tablespoons brown sugar |
| 2 | cups unbleached all-purpose flour |
| 2 | teaspoons baking powder |
| 1 | teaspoons baking soda |
| 1 | teaspoon salt |
| ½ | teaspoon cinnamon |

## Buttermilk

FOR A QUICK BUTTERMILK SUBSTITUTE, ADD 1 TABLESPOON WHITE VINEGAR TO 1 CUP MILK AND LET SIT FOR 5 TO 10 MINUTES.

PREHEAT WAFFLE IRON and when hot spray with non-stick spray. Whisk together the eggs, buttermilk, Vanilla Bean Olive Oil, and brown sugar.

Add combined remaining dry ingredients. Mix until just combined.

Pour by half cupfuls into the hot waffle iron and cook until golden brown. Serve with a large scoop of your favorite ice cream or gelato and garnish with fruit as desired, or with syrup and butter for breakfast.

# INDEX

# Gourmet Grilled Cheese

BRUSH BREAD WITH EXTRA VIRGIN OLIVE OIL INSTEAD OF BUTTER FOR GRILLED CHEESE SANDWICHES. FOR THE GOURMET VERSION, ADD FRESH SLICED TOMATOES AND FRESH BASIL LEAVES TO THE SANDWICH AFTER GRILLING. DELICIOUS!

# Old-Fashioned Popcorn

POUR A THIN LAYER OF EXTRA VIRGIN OLIVE OIL IN A LARGE POT AND ADD 3 POPCORN KERNELS. HEAT OVER HIGH HEAT, AND WHEN THESE 3 KERNELS POP, ADD POPCORN IN A SINGLE LAYER TO COVER THE BOTTOM OF THE POT. WHEN ALL THE KERNELS ARE POPPED, ADD SALT TO TASTE. NO NEED FOR BUTTER! ALSO FUN TO TRY WITH DIFFERENT FLAVORED OILS: QCOM CHILI OLIVE OIL AND QCOM TRUFFLE OLIVE OIL ARE A COUPLE OF OUR FAVORITES.

# EVOO Eggs

COOK FRIED OR SCRAMBLED EGGS IN OLIVE OIL: YOU CAN USE EVOO OR TRY QCOM CHILI OLIVE OIL OR QCOM GARLIC OLIVE OIL FOR A TASTY CHANGE OF PACE.

# TIPS FOR USING OLIVE OIL

# Virign Skin

RUB A LITTLE EXTRA VIRGIN OLIVE OIL DIRECTLY INTO YOUR SKIN FOR AN ANCIENT, AND VERY EFFECTIVE MOISTURIZER. NO WORRIES ABOUT CHEMICAL ADDITIVES OR ALLERGENIC INGREDIENTS HERE, JUST NATURAL ANTIOXIDANTS AND VITAMINS! ADD ESSENTIAL OILS FOR ADDED BENEFITS AND WONDERFUL AROMAS, OR TRY OUR LINE OF OLIVE OIL SKIN CARE PRODUCTS.

# The Squeaky Hinge Gets the Oil

APPLY A FEW DROPS OF OLIVE OIL TO QUIET A SQUEAKING HINGE.

# Glistening Wood

COMBINE ONE CUP OF OLIVE OIL WITH A ¼ CUP OF WHITE VINEGAR. POUR INTO A CLEAN SPRAY BOTTLE FOR A NON-TOXIC, ENVIRONMENTALLY-FRIENDLY WOOD FURNITURE CLEANER! SPRAY ON A CLEAN SOFT CLOTH (NOT DIRECTLY ONTO THE FURNITURE) AND WORK INTO THE WOOD, WIPING WITH THE GRAIN.

## BUTTER TO OLIVE OIL CONVERSION CHART

| BUTTER/MARGARINE > | OLIVE OIL |
| --- | --- |
| 1 TEASPOON | 3/4 TEASPOON |
| 1 TABLESPOON | 2 1/4 TEASPOONS |
| 2 TABLESPOONS | 1 1/2 TABLESPOONS |
| 1/4 CUP | 3 TABLESPOONS |
| 1/3 CUP | 1/4 CUP |
| 1/2 CUP | 1/4 CUP + 2 TABLESPOONS |
| 2/3 CUP | 1/2 CUP |
| 3/4 CUP | 1/2 CUP + 1 TABLESPOON |
| 1 CUP | 3/4 CUP |